CUBA CLIMBING

AF496585

QUICKDRAW
PUBLICATIONS

BY ANÍBAL FERNÁNDEZ & ARMANDO MENOCAL

CUBA CLIMBING

POSTAL ADDRESS
PO Box 5313
Squamish, BC V8B 0C2
Canada

CONTACT US
(604) 892-9271
info@quickdrawpublications.com
www.quickdrawpublications.com

Quickdraw Publications is constantly expanding our range of guidebooks. If you have a manuscript or an idea for a book, or would like to find out more about our company, please get in touch.

Designed and typeset in Canada; printed and bound in Hong Kong.

FIRST EDITION

INTERNATIONAL STANDARD BOOK NUMBER
ISBN 978-0-9732593-6-0

AUTHORS
Aníbal Fernández & Armando Menocal

PHOTOGRAPHY
All photographs by the authors unless otherwise noted. Front cover photograph of *Mucho Pumpito* by Andrew Burr. Back cover photographs of *The Wasp Factory* and palms by Andrew Burr. Back cover photo of car by Marc Pagani. Back cover photograph of beverage by "José The Cuban". Photograph this page by Andrew Burr.

Give Us Your Feedback

Due to the changeable nature of rock climbing, guidebooks often become outdated soon after publication. To help alleviate this problem, we've created **Cubaclimbing.com** to provide corrections, updates and the latest travel information for climbers. To help improve everyone's climbing experience in Cuba, we need your feedback! After using this guidebook, please help us by providing information about your experiences. We welcome suggestions and corrections to the route information as well as changes to any photographs or maps. And, of course, if you establish a new climb, please let us know. Thank you for helping to improve climbing in Cuba.

Disclaimer

Read this before you use this book! Rock climbing is a sport with inherent risks. Participating in rock climbing may result in injury or death.

This guidebook is intended for climbers with a degree of ability and experience. The terrain described within is dangerous and requires a high level of fitness and technical expertise to negotiate. This guidebook is a compilation of information from several sources. As a result the authors cannot confirm the accuracy of any specific detail. Difficulty ratings are subjective and may vary depending on your own personal experience and the conditions of the climb. There may be misinformation in regards to route descriptions, conditions, difficulties or any other detail. This guidebook does not give the user the right to access any terrain described within. The land owner or land manager may limit access to any part of an area at any time. It is your responsibility to adhere to all closures.

ACKNOWLEDGEMENTS

We would like to thank all the people who have supported climbing in Cuba over the years, thus making it possible for us to write this book. Without the *guajiros* and residents of Viñales, who hosted us for years and welcomed climbing into their world, there would be nothing to report. In particular, we want to express our gratitude to the families of Oscar Jaime and Miguel Angel Catalá, who took us into their homes and hearts and made us one of their own. Also, a big thanks goes out to Raúl Reyes and all the farmers who graciously let us use their land without asking for anything in return.

We would also like to acknowledge all of the first ascensionists who left their mark (and sweat) on the walls of Viñales Valley. Xabi Alvarez, David Brasco, Cameron Cross, Vitalio Echazábal, Tim Emmett, Neil Gresham, Seb Grieve, Paul Laperrière, Alberto Leivas, Craig Luebben, Jorge "El Gato" Luis, Jorge Mederos, Josué Millo, Abel Pérez, David Ryan, Reiniel Sosa and Edu Viana are just a few of the names behind the many routes, and to them go our thanks and apologies for any mistakes we've made in reporting their climbs. Also, much appreciation goes out to the companies and individuals who defied politics, borders and custom taxes to donate the gear necessary for the Cubans to start climbing and developing routes – you made a huge difference in many people's lives.

To all the individuals who shared information and their great photographs, a special thanks. In particular, we are indebted to Andy Burr, Jimmy Chin, Yarobys García, Alan Hamilton, Ben Iseman, "José The Cuban", Fernando Nuñez, Marc Pagani, Mike Robertson, Beth Wald and Peter Winter for donating so much and for believing in this project from the very beginning. Thanks to Daniel Duane, Neil Gresham, Craig Luebben and Timmy O'Neill for writing great perspectives on their Cuban experiences, which added valuable depth to the book. Thanks also to our editor and publisher, Marc Bourdon of Quickdraw Publications, for putting a great book together from the pile of drawings and CDs we sent to his mailbox.

We would particularly thank our friends and families for so much support and understanding through years of putting the important things aside for the selfish pursuit of climbing. Aníbal adds his personal thanks to his mother who bought him his first proper climbing harness, to his father who inspired him to write, and to his wife for all her love and patience.

"I dedicate this book to my friends Vity, Mede and Abel, who shared my dreams and my ropes."   ~Aníbal Fernández

TABLE OF CONTENTS

INTRODUCTION

"Rock is rock it's true, but climbing in Cuba isn't like climbing in any other place. Climbing in Cuba is as much about Cuba as it is about climbing." With these words, author Jonny Miles captured the true essence of climbing in Cuba. The country conjures up visions of romance, music, beauty and intrigue. Upon "discovering" Cuba on October 27, 1492, Christopher Columbus described the island as "the most beautiful thing human eyes could ever behold". Ernest Hemingway, Winston Churchill and Graham Greene have all fallen in love with Cuba.

Few visitors to Cuba come away equivocal. Most become passionate about Cuba; it reaches into you emotionally. The Cuban people are sensual, musical and mystical; they draw you in. They shout across courtyards and streets every detail of their daily emotions and calamities. It's "in-your-face" living and not for the timid or bashful. Use this book to find the climbs, but make sure to explore the country and its people – a true adventure awaits.

MAD ROCK
MadRockClimbing.Com

MAD ROCK
Beta
$69.95 USD

Ultra Light Quick Draw
$13.95 USD

MAD ROCK
SCIENCE FRICTION
Con-Flict
$99.95 USD

WELCOME TO CUBA

The focus of rock climbing activity in Cuba is the Valle de Viñales in the western, mountainous province of Pinar del Río. This valley has that combination of high quality rock, accessibility and ambience to suggest that Cuba could become one of the top sport climbing destinations in the world. The climbing is superlative; cranking jugs, pockets and stalactites in chiselled karst limestone on improbable lines through stunning overhangs leaves one breathless.

The Valle de Viñales is now a national park and a World Heritage Site, touted as the most spectacular scenery in all of Cuba. Overhanging limestone faces on 300-metre freestanding crags called "mogotes" rise above traditional thatch-roofed Cuban houses and red-soiled tobacco farms. Western Cuba is a one-hour flight from Cancun, only a little longer from Canada or Europe and home to the best limestone this side of Thailand. It has recently seen an influx of leading climbers, such as Lynn Hill, Timmy O'Neil and Neil Gresham, and the development of a strong contingent of Cuban climbers, who are eager to climb with visitors.

The mountains around Viñales now have over 250 routes (300 pitches of climbing) with potential for hundreds more. Perfect climbing days, mild weather and everything from isolated beaches to caving and cockfights on rest days make for a one-of-a-kind vacation. Add an exciting, sensuous nightlife, the gregarious, vivacious Cuban people and the country may already be the best outdoor adventure experience anywhere.

GEOGRAPHY

The Republic of Cuba is an island nation with three major water bodies lapping at its shores: the Caribbean Sea, the Gulf of Mexico and the Atlantic Ocean. The country consists of the long, curved island of Cuba, the small, round Isla de la Juventud and several archipelagos (chains or clusters of islands that are formed tectonically). Geographically, Cuba is located south of the eastern United States and The Bahamas, west of Haiti, east of Mexico and north of the Cayman Islands and Jamaica.

This subtropical country is home to over 11 million people, making it the most populated insular nation in the Caribbean. The main island constitutes most of the nation's land area and, at 1233 kilometres long, is the 17th largest island in the world. Havana (Cuba's capital) is the largest city in the country and is a bustling port located along the northern coastline, approximately 170 kilometres southwest of Key West, Florida.

Forested mountains make up a quarter of Cuba's territory, and fertile plains used for growing sugarcane or grazing cattle make up much of the rest. Cuba has almost 6000 kilometres of coastline with close to 300 natural beaches. Northern beaches tend to have exquisite white sand and rolling surf, while southern beaches tend to be darker, warmer and less prone to the cold fronts that sweep across the north.

At a glance...

Capital: Havana
Population: 11 423 952
Official Language: Spanish

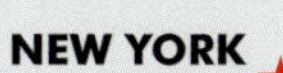

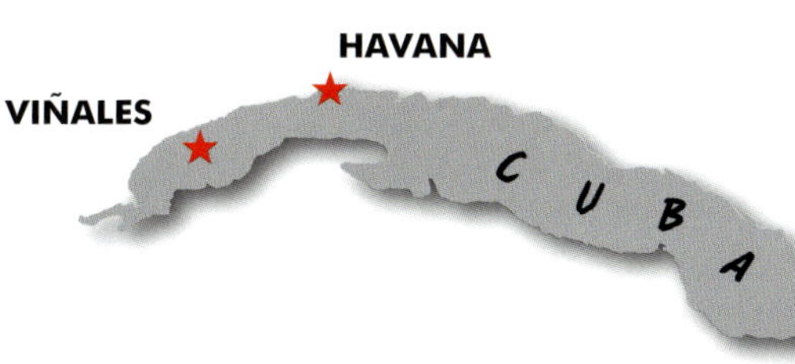

FLORA & FAUNA

Cuba, like most islands, is not home to large native animals. With the limited resources an island provides, it is usually more convenient to stay small. However, the diversity of birds, reptiles, amphibians and invertebrates can be mind-boggling, and many of these creatures are endemic to Cuba; that is, they are found nowhere else on earth.

The karst mountains of Sierra de los Organos that surround Viñales form an "island within an island". The lack of superficial water and the rocky nature of the pincushion hills, or *mogotes,* have long kept people from settling in the region. The mogotes form fortresses that have created a singular biodiversity, including species that are highly specialized to live in the limestone cliffs and thus are unique to the area. Rock iguanas, dozens of small lizards, tree frogs, snakes (none poisonous), snails and countless arthropods spend their lives scrawling around the porous rock looking for rainwater that collects in the many holes. All these creatures occupy different niches, from the xerophytic summits punished by the sun to the shady humid forests that form deep in the *hoyos* (sunken holes left by collapsed caves).

Similarly, species of bats inhabit the many caves and a good selection of endemic and

Royal Palms

migrant birds wander around the vegetation. In the Viñales area, look for the bee hummingbird, the smallest bird in the world, or the tocororo, Cuba's national bird bearing the colours of the Cuban flag: red, white and blue (see page 66).

The area has just one native mammal of size, the rat-like rodent jutía. These animals are more closely related to the capybaras and agoutis of South America than to European rats, but their appearance does discourage many foreigners from trying this local delicacy. Cuban farmers have hunted jutías for many years and still explore the interior of the mogotes for prey, but today jutías are protected by law, although poaching is not uncommon. At least two different species are found in Viñales: the rock loving Conga and the tree-hugging Carabali, both timid, nocturnal creatures that you would be very lucky to catch a glimpse of.

Many plants are also endemic to this landscape, including cacti, bromeliads and delicate orchids. Perching dragos, yagrumas, various ficus and palms are the signature trees of the area. A primitive dwarf palm, the Palma Corcho, has also selected this valley to inhabit since the age of the dinosaurs and some can be seen on the road to El Campismo.

This unique combination of animals and plants is as fragile as it is beautiful. Climbers who use this magnificent mogote environment should act responsibly and minimize disturbance.

Belly (Corojo) Palm

GEOLOGY

At first glance, the Viñales Valley appears to be a jagged landscape of rocky formations containing carved-out vaults and caverns that drip with stalactites and bulge with tufas. These features pack together to form rounded, jungle-covered hummocks (*mogotes*) and deep holes (*hoyos*). The first explorers that saw this range from the north coast of Cuba called it "Sierra de los Organos" because the towering mountains resembled organ pipes.

In geological terms, this area is known as a "karst landscape" and the mogotes around Viñales constitute one of the most advanced karst formations on the planet. Karst is a phenomenon that occurs when water dissolves relatively soft rocks, such as limestone or dolomite, to create caves, caverns and underground rivers; generally sculpting the rock in a very particular way. The most evolved karst landscapes are in areas of Southeast Asia, China, South America and the Caribbean, places with lots of limestone and high precipitation, year-round.

The combination of porous rock and abundant water allow the karst process to root and grow; in Viñales, this growth has been ferocious. Virtually all of the crags described in this book, at some point in their geological history, were part of an underground gallery of caves that grew for miles. These caverns formed intricate webs that eventually collapsed under their own weight, leaving behind incredible, organically-shaped labyrinths of rock.

For climbers, the resulting features from this process offer a unique three-dimensional canvas on which to paint improbable routes up and through hanging chandeliers and immense overhangs. In Cuba's overhead caverns, the bulging tufas and dangling stalactites are suspended all around as one climbs, sometimes offering a saving rest or "stem" in the most exposed position believable! These drop-forged features range from handhold-sized stilettos to giant inverted statuary.

Figure 1 *Limestone originates at the bottom of the sea. Layers of sediment and organic matter get deposited and compressed over time to form a sedimentary rock that often includes many fossils. This stone eventually gets thrust upward via tectonic movement and, as the rock is lifted, forms cracks that allow rain to percolate through. Thus begins the process of erosion.*

Figure 2 *Rain dissolves rock on its way through the cracks, which opens up small caves. Sediment starts leaching through the rock and gets deposited lower down in the form of small stalactites. The river starts to erode the bottom of the monolith.*

FIGURE 1
rain
cracks
limestone
limestone

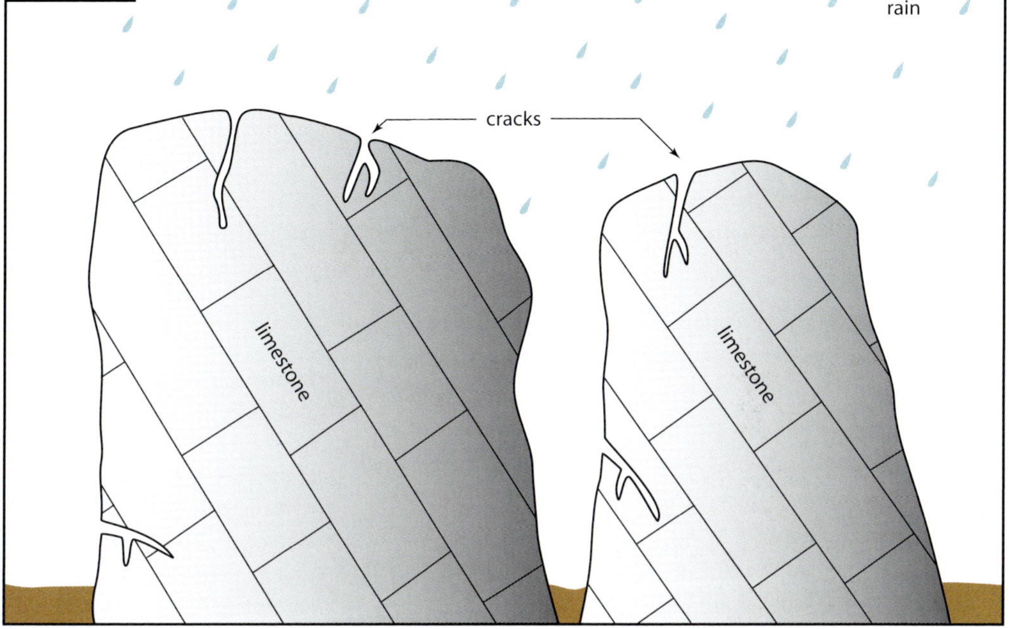

FIGURE 2
rain
caves
"hoyo"
limestone
limestone
cave
river

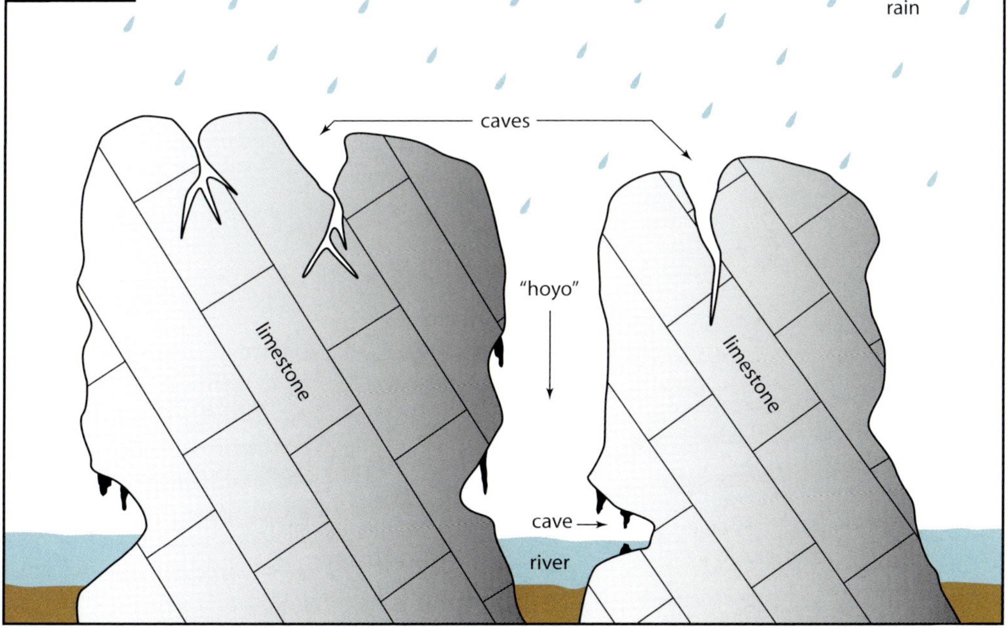

Water defines the climbing here, forming the actual walls and major formations. Water also creates the details and variety of textures, shapes and colours that give the area a unique diversity. Rain falls directly over the structural rock and wears away the stone, slowly sharpening it into razors and leaving delicate, yet stout, lattices and honeycombs. So, if the rock is less than vertical (usually the grey limestone), expect sharp holds and technical climbing.

The sediments from the sharpening process run through cracks and mix with other minerals, getting deposited farther down the cliff in caves and overhangs. Here, the sediments form the classic limestone overhang features – stalactites and tufas – as well as three-dimensional "crusts". These crusts form climber-friendly incuts, buckets and pockets, as well as an overflow stone that leaves behind amazing slot features, perfect for a thread, hand or knee. In the caves, there are few pockmarks, dimples, or crimps – the features aren't tiny, they're supersized!

Figure 3 *Continued erosion by water causes caverns and vertical caves to form. Large sections of rock crumble and collapse creating new waterways. Many secondary formations appear, such as stalactites on the ceilings and stalagmites on the ground.*

Figure 4 *Lots of caverns collapse creating boulder talus at the base of the walls. The collapsing caverns also expose big overhangs, which are perfect for climbing. The river retires leaving big, dry caverns that sometimes connect with vertical caves.*

FIGURE 3

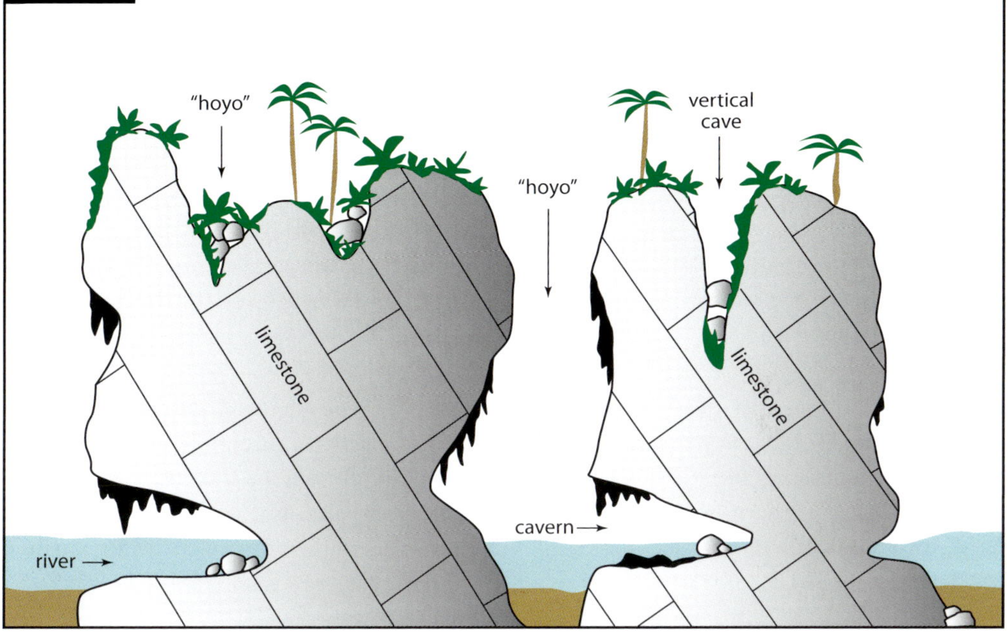

FIGURE 4

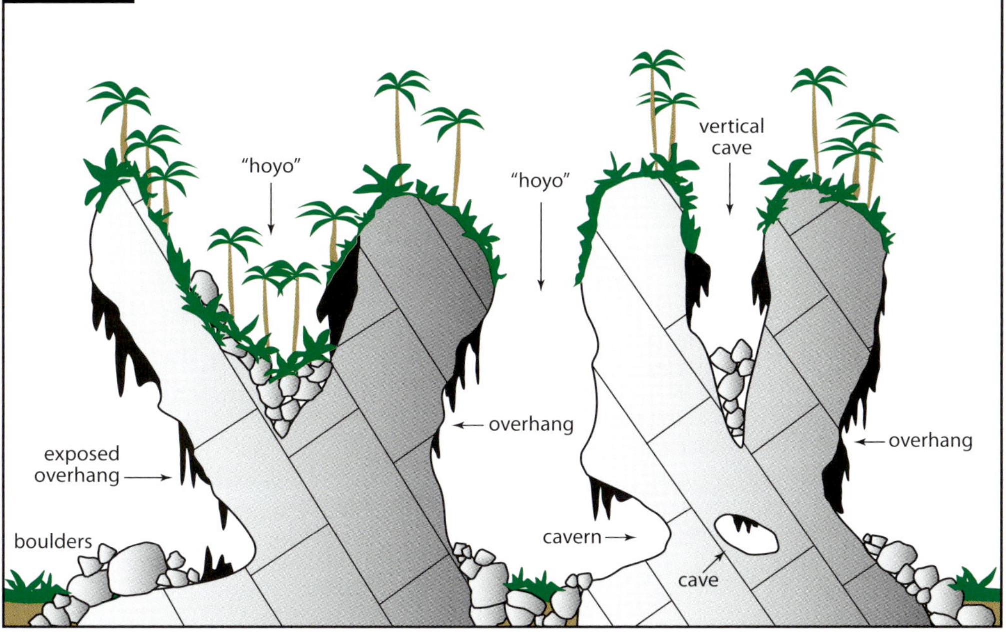

PLANNING YOUR TRIP

Websites

For the latest information on travelling to Cuba, be sure to visit Cubaclimbing.com. This website was created with travelling climbers in mind and contains excellent logistical information for planning a trip, including links to almost every climbing article written about Cuba. The young Cuban climbers in Viñales have also created a useful website, Escaladaencuba.com. It's a great source for last minute climbing news. For a comprehensive link to other Cuba-related websites, ranging from arts and culture to news and newsgroups, visit the following web address: http://www.lanic.utexas.edu/la/cb/cuba/.

Books

Cuba is a major tourist destination and there are many good travel guidebooks available including Bradt, Eyewitness, Fodors, Footprint, Insight, Lonely Planet and Rough Guides. Our recommendation is the Cuba Moon Handbook. Its author, Christopher Baker, has written the most outlandish, yet revealing and thought-provoking adventure book on Cuba, *Mi Moto Fidel*, about his 3-month exploration of the island on a 1000 CC, Paris-Dakar, BMW motorcycle.

© ANDREW BURR

Climate

Cuba's subtropical climate is ideal for adventure seekers looking for a climbing vacation in a unique country with beautiful beaches. Although it may feel hot to some winter-hardened northerners, the weather in Cuba is far from the muggy, sweat-box climbing conditions of Southeast Asia. This is primarily due to the country-wide influence of the moderating, gentle Northeast Trade Winds that help cool the air and lower humidity. Although temperature fluctuations are rather minimal throughout the year, Cuban weather can be loosely categorized into two "seasons": a warm, rainy summer (May–October) and a dry winter (November–April) with slightly cooler temperatures. Additionally, intense tropical storms (hurricanes) may affect Cuba's weather and the threat lasts from June–November. If there are storms, the most intense hurricanes usually pass through in September and early October.

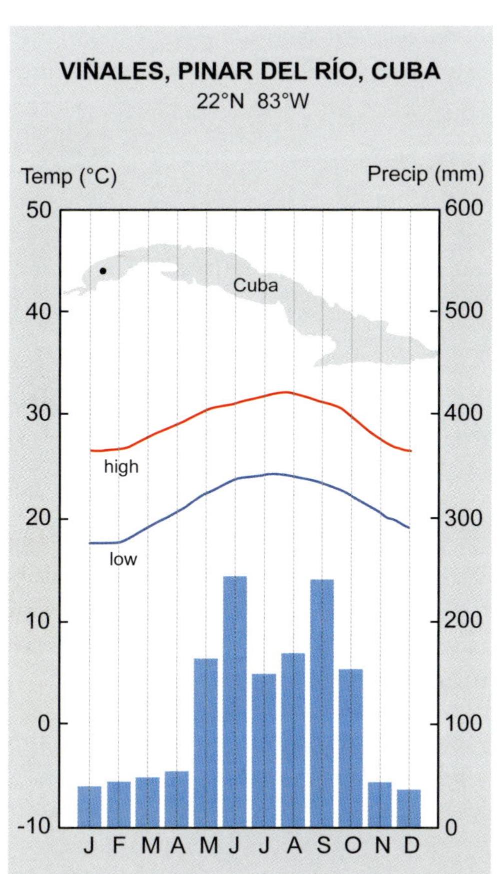

When to Go

Due to the abundance of overhangs and north-facing walls, it's possible to climb at any time of the year, but the very best conditions occur during winter. The coolest months are December, January and February where nights can be downright chilly; sweaters and fleece jackets are advised. Hurricane season, especially the tail-end months of October and November, can also provide good climbing conditions as can March and April, but the probability of precipitation starts to rise as the rainy season approaches. See Figure 1 for more specific climate data.

Figure 1 *Average monthly rainfall and temperature (high and low) for the village of Viñales, Pinar del Río Province, Cuba.*

Gear Basics

You can climb in Viñales for a couple of days with just a dozen quickdraws and a 60-metre rope. You'll be finished packing if you throw in a couple of T-shirts, some shorts, mosquito repellent and sunscreen. Excessive clothing is unnecessary as any *casa particular* (privately run house accommodation) will wash your clothes as soon as they hit the floor. Also, it's warm enough to make rain gear pretty much dispensable. Note that a few nights between January and February might get cool enough to warrant bringing a sweater or fleece jacket.

Planning on staying longer? Bring a second 60-metre rope to rappel the multi-pitch sport climbs (e.g. *Mucho Pumpito*) and throw in some extra carabiners and slings for building anchors, threading tufas and replacing worn rappel webbing. The majority of multi-pitch routes can be climbed with a maximum of 16 quickdraws and a rack of cams is pretty much unnecessary. The few gear climbs that do exist are often of poor quality and rarely get climbed; most are slowly getting retrobolted.

In summary, sport climbing in the tropics does not require much, which is a real bonus in this era of disappearing baggage weight allowance.

Gear Donations

To sustain the local climbers, please pack excess climbing gear and leave it behind. The Cubans *need* climbing equipment; it's impossible to get it locally. The majority of visitors now follow the tradition initiated in 1998 by Colombian climber, Alberto Morales, who left his rack, ropes, shoes and harness in Cuba when he left. Try it – you will feel very gratified. In order to understand what is useful, here are some suggestions:

❑ Regarding personal gear, most useful are the basics: shoes, harnesses, ropes, chalk and packs. However, the single biggest need to propel Cuban climbing forward is bolts and hangers. If you do go to the trouble, please bring stainless steel or titanium hardware, with studs at least three inches long by three eights of an inch in diameter.

❑ The Cubans, like the rest of us, really love climbing accessories: shorts, T-shirts, hats, climbing magazines and posters.

❑ For clothing, shoes and harnesses, small sizes are best. We don't know a single Cuban climber who uses a large harness. The local kids need gear, too.

❑ All equipment in good condition is welcome, but please don't bring heavily worn gear or old clothes. It's extra work to bring gear to Cuba, so it's a shame to bring junk like old hexes, faded slings and ripped shoes.

❑ Although you may donate your gear as you please, we recommend that you leave it with one of the prominent local climbers who will see that it finds the best home possible. Check Cubaclimbing.com for the latest recommended contact.

Packing for Route Exploration

If you plan to explore new terrain and develop routes on the many unclimbed walls, your luggage is going to get heavy! You'll need the usual kit: rack, bolts, hooks, Tricams, hangers, drill and batteries. Additionally, bring tough pants, long-sleeved shirts and gloves. Use these for protection against the thorns and *guao* (Cuba's version of poison ivy) encountered while trashing through the jungle in search of the promised land. While on the wall, garden clippers, saws, wire brushes and machetes may be very useful for clearing stubborn vegetation. Note that no self-respecting *campesino* would ever be caught dead without a machete in Cuba, but good ones are no longer easily purchased on the island.

If you do go to the trouble of developing new routes, please contact us with the details for inclusion in future editions of this guide.

Come prepared *A simple cragging pack will do for most visitors (left), but route exploration and wasp "clearing" requires special equipment (right).*

Flights

There are flights to Cuba from the Caribbean, Latin America, Canada, and Europe. Canada has the best deals; some Canadian charters include air, room and food. Sometimes these packages are so inexpensive that it's worthwhile to purchase them for the flight alone and blow-off the resort hotel and its bad food once you arrive. Sometimes, the cheapest flights to Cuba are on Cubana, the state-run carrier that occasionally flies ancient and scary Soviet-era planes. For a comprehensive list of departure cities, visit Anashtravel.com. To book Cancun–Havana flights, contact the Cuban travel specialists, Víajes Divermex, through their website Divermex.com.

Touchdown *Cuban flag outside Havana's airport.*

Special Consideration for United States Visitors

For almost 50 years, Cuban travel for United States citizens and residents has been limited by the United States government due to Cold War trade and travel restrictions. Regular, direct flights from major United States cities are only available to restricted categories of visitors, such as Cuban-Americans, full-time journalists and government officials. All other citizens and residents may travel to Cuba, but only through a third country, such as Canada, Mexico or The Bahamas. Doing so is easy and relatively risk-free, but is still, technically, illegal. At the time of this writing, the United States travel policies for Cuba did seem likely to change. Check Cubaclimbing.com and other Internet resources for the latest travel information and tips.

Travel Documents

Cuba welcomes tourists and all travel is unrestricted. Visitors entering the country need a passport (valid for at least six additional months), an onward airline ticket and a *tarjeta de turista* (tourist card); visas are unnecessary. Travel agents and airlines sell tourist cards and it's best to obtain one ahead of time to avoid problems. Upon arrival, Cuban immigration will stamp your card (not your passport), thus allowing a stay of 30 days. This period can be extended by another 30 days for a small fee. Be sure to keep this card in a safe place as you will need it to board your flight home.

Money

Two currencies currently circulate throughout Cuba – the peso (CUP) used by Cubans, and the convertible peso (CUC) used by travellers (one peso is worth about $\frac{1}{25}$ a convertible peso, or about four pennies). Common foreign currencies, such as Canadian dollars, Euros and British pounds, are all easily exchanged at banks and exchange booths, but prepare to pay an 8% government-imposed exchange fee. U.S. dollars are also convertible, but incur an additional 10% fee. Theoretically, it is best to convert U.S. dollars to another currency beforehand; however, multiple exchanges with commissions usually cancel out any potential savings. The vocabulary of money is often more confusing than the money itself. In practice, nearly everything a tourist needs to purchase is priced in convertible pesos, which are commonly referred to as "chavitos". Cubans, however, will sometimes say, for example, that something is "un peso", meaning one chavito. To make this even more confusing, the United States dollar was the official currency for a decade and Cubans still say "dolares" to mean chavitos. Context is the key: if buying a beer, it is about one dollar, even if quoted "un peso, un dolar, or un chavito". Finally, since CUCs are useless outside Cuba you should reverse-exchange any remaining currency at the airport before leaving.

ATMs

Automatic teller machines are common and reliable in Havana and Santiago, but elsewhere they may not be dependable, despite their availability. If they work and you get cash, consider yourself lucky. U.S. bank cards **will not** work so U.S. visitors should ensure they have **plenty of cash** for the duration of their trip.

Credit Cards, Travellers Cheques & Security

Credit cards are useful in Cuba (Visa is the most accepted), but there is an 8% commission charged to them and cards issued by United States banks **are not** accepted in Cuba due to the trade embargo. Carrying travellers cheques is an option, but they can be difficult and expensive to cash at times. Finally, cruising around with a big wad of bills in your pocket is definitely not recommended. As a general rule, carry only the cash you need for the day and never walk around with your passport.

HAVANA AT A GLANCE

Since most visitors travel through Havana on their way to Viñales, a brief introduction to the city is included here. Many excellent travel guides to Havana are available, which expand greatly on the following information.

History

Havana (la Habana) is the biggest city in the Caribbean as well as the political and cultural capital of Cuba. It was founded in 1515 by the Spanish conquistador Diego Velazquez and named "San Cristobal de la La Habana", likely after the native American chief, Habaguanex, that controlled the area at the time. A more romantic, but unconfirmed, version of the story has the city named for the chief's beautiful daughter, Habana.

This great harbour city was one of the most important ports during the Spanish conquest of the Americas. Its strategic position also made it desirable for other nations and Havana received numerous attacks over the years, including effective assaults from the British who took control of the city for almost a year during the 18th century. Spain was able to negotiate its return in exchange for Florida, and the city remained under Spanish control until the beginning of the 20th century. In 1898, Cuba gained independence from Spain and entered a new republican era under the "supervision" of the United States. The next 50 years brought economic development; hotels, casinos and residences were built to support a new affluence based on high sugar prices and tourism that exploited sex, booze and gambling. Havana became a playground where stars and gangsters mingled – the beautiful setting combined with the architecture and rich culture made it into one of the most seductive cities of the Americas. Graham Greene, Ernest Hemingway, Frederico García Lorca and many others fell for it and Havana was dubbed the "Paris of the Caribbean", with the largest middle-class of any country in Latin America.

After the revolution of 1959, Havana went through great changes. All gambling stopped, all foreign property was nationalized and private businesses were replaced by a state-controlled economy based on the Soviet model. The harsh economical years that followed the revolution left the city in the dilapidated condition found today. Efforts are now being made to rescue Havana from imminent degradation, but progress is slow and only focused on select neighbourhoods.

Nevertheless, Havana remains a vibrant place full of colourful people – a timeless city that wears its scars and wrinkles with great pride. Colonial, neoclassical, baroque and eclectic architecture all mix to form the many fascinating neighbourhoods. Museums and galleries abound, and old American cars rumble around the streets providing a dated, yet noble, rhythm to this great city.

El Malecón *Dramatic coastline (bottom) and architecture (top) frame the north side of Havana.*

What to do?

The most popular regions of the city for tourists are the historic streets of La Habana Vieja (Old Havana) and the bustling shopping district of Centro Habana. Adjacent to La Habana Vieja is the famous and well-photographed Havana waterfront, where the city really boils with life – markets, bars and plazas crowd the walkways and the ancient Spanish fortress, El Morro, looms over the entrance to the harbour. The districts of Vedado, Playa and Miramar, offer a more relaxing experience with lots of green grass and fewer tourists. The best music clubs, including those playing Latin Jazz, are found in these areas. Here is a two-day sightseeing list:

- ❑ Tour the fortresses of San Carlos de la Cabaña and El Morro.
- ❑ Tour historic La Habana Vieja.
- ❑ Wander along the waterfront.
- ❑ Visit the Museo de Bellas Artes.
- ❑ Visit Casa de la Musica Habana (a great Cuban music venue).

Where to stay?

Travel guides to Cuba are chock full of information on accommodation, along with recommendations for Havana. For specific climber-friendly options, see the general accommodation section starting on page 30.

Transportation

Havana's public transportation system is somewhat unreliable – the buses and "camellos" are hot and crowded. For tourists, the best way to get around the city is to walk, use cabs, "cocotaxis" (scooters) or "bicitaxis". If visiting for more than a few days, consider renting a car or buying a bike. To arrange a cab, call Panataxi Habana at 55 54 56.

Where to eat?

Many tourists eat at their hotel or *casa particular*, but other options exist, including state-run restaurants, *paladares* (private restaurants) and street vendors. See the Food & Drink section starting on page 34 for more information. Havana recommendations:

Restaurants

- ❑ La Bodeguita del Medio (Empedrado #206, Habana Vieja)
- ❑ La Mina, Obispo (#111, Habana Vieja)
- ❑ El Aljibe (Ave 7ma and 24, Miramar)
- ❑ Los 12 Apostoles (El Morro Castle)
- ❑ El Palenque (Calle 17 & 190, Miramar)

Paladares

- ❑ La Guarida (Concordia #418, Centro Habana)
- ❑ Huron Azul (Humbolt #153, Centro Habana)
- ❑ Amor (Calle 23 #759, Vedado)
- ❑ Gringo Viejo (Calle 21 #453, Vedado)
- ❑ La Cocina de Lilliam (Calle 48 #1311, Miramar)

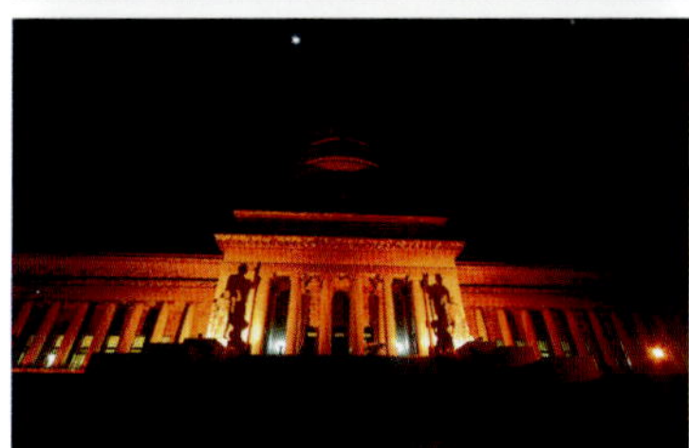

City Images *Clockwise from bottom left: Gran Teatro de La Habana; "cocotaxis" in La Habana Vieja; musician strumming a "tres" (a Cuban instrument similar to a guitar); Ernesto "Che" Guevara memorial near Plaza de la Revolución; El Capitolio at night; street performers in La Habana Vieja.*

◎ MARC PAGANI

ACCOMMODATION

In Cuba, all hotels are controlled by the government and rooms in private houses are heavily taxed. Because of this, accommodation prices are fairly inflexible, making bargain-basement travel difficult at best. To top it off, it's virtually impossible to camp out and cook due to the absence of campgrounds and the difficulty of buying staple foods. All is not lost, however. The prices on the existing accommodation options are fairly moderate by Western standards, and Cuba has lovely *casas particulares.*

Private Rooms (*Casas Particulares*)

© MIKE ROBERTSON

Cuba's charm is its people and the quickest way to meet them is to rent a room in one of their homes, the *casas particulares.* Almost any is better than a hotel and the homes are typically the most economical accommodation option ($15–35 CUC per room per day). Staying in a *casa particular* is a chance to experience genuine Cuban culture as you'll be immersed in a Cuban family's life for the length of your stay. The nature of the accommodation varies from single rooms with shared baths to private bungalows or apartments. Breakfast and dinner are typically provided for an additional fee (sometimes negotiable in Viñales) and most owners will expect you to book these meals – they count on it to make ends meet. Note that it's considered very bad form to stay in one house and eat at another.

Regarding reservations, it's wise to secure one for the first night in Havana (at least) and use the details to fill in your tourist card at the airport. Without any sort of accommodation reservation, Cuban Immigration may compel you to pay for a government hotel on the spot. If calling to make a reservation at a *casa particular*, please note that it's helpful to speak a little Spanish as you'll be calling a private home, not a reception desk. A final cautionary note: bad experiences with *casas particulares* are rare, but is a competitive business that attracts some scams. Taxi drivers, "guides", or other owners may try to take you to an alternative house, claiming the one you booked is full or closed. Also, be wary of anyone offering to "guide" you to your pre-booked house. This person will likely try to extract a "finders fee" from the *casa*, which will then be charged back to you.

Hundreds of families rent rooms in Havana and Viñales, but we recommend only a few because we know the owners will help you, even if they are already booked:

❑ Esther Cardoso (Havana): Esther has a beautifully reconstructed colonial home, with high ceilings, balconies and shuttered windows. The *casa* is in Centro Habana, on the edge of Habana Vieja, and is exceptionally convenient for sightseeing. As an actress and teacher, Esther's living room can include a true cross-section of modern Cuban culture. Aguila #367, e/Neptuno y San Miguel, Centro Habana. Phone: 53-7-862-0401, esther-cardoso@hotmail.com, esthercv2551@cubarte.cult.cu.

❑ Ana María Fariñas (Havana): This house is a favourite with climbers. It has reasonable prices, is in a genuine Cuban neighborhood with few tourists, and is located close to the bus terminal, which makes it a great place to stay when in transit to Viñales. Ana María speaks English and has many contacts. Salvador Allende (Carlos Tercero) No. 1005, e/ Requena y Almendares, Plaza. Phone: 53-7-878-2946, mati2k@lare.ch.gov.cu, anamaria@isdi.co.cu.

Casa Oscar

Phone: 53-4-869-5516
Email: oscar.jaime59@gmail.com

Thumbs Up *Oscar Jaime and his family welcome you to Viñales.*

❏ Oscar Jaime Rodriguez (Viñales): This *casa particular* has become the climbers' basecamp in Viñales; the house, amenities and food are all excellent. Oscar welcomes visitors with open arms and acts as host, friend and protector while you stay in his village. The compound of several houses includes grandparents, brothers, sisters, nieces, nephews and cousins. If Oscar is booked, he'll ensure that a quality alternative is made available. Call ahead to make a reservation and provide details of your arrival. Adela Azcuy #43, oscar.jaime59@gmail.com, phone: 53-4-869-5516.

For the sake of being comprehensive, we've described the other potential accommodation options for visits to Cuba.

Camping

Despite the pleasures of staying in *casas particulares*, the question most asked by climbers is, "What about camping?" For them, there is "Casa Gringo", a cave-camp established by Craig Luebben on his route *Mr. Mogote*. To find it, walk four kilometres north of town, locate a trail through the jungle to the base, and then complete a 40-metre free-hanging jumar to the cave. In other words, what most travellers think of as "camping" is very rare in Cuba; however, some climbers have camped on farms before, with the permission of the owner. Realistically, this is the safest and most reliable option, if you must camp.

Campismos

In Cuba, *campismos* typically consist of a compound of small bungalows along with some amenities. They can be very popular with local Cubans on weekends, but might be deserted, or even closed, during the week. Viñales has one *campismo*, which is on the road to Mogotes Dos Hermanos, about five kilometres from town. It features small cottages with four or six beds, a central cafeteria and a pool. To make this option practical, you'll likely need a car or a bike.

Hotels

In Cuba, there is an abundance of government-run hotels, but they are primarily focused in the major tourist areas, like Varadero. There are a few hotel options close to Viñales

Hotel Los Jasmines *This hotel features some nice amenities, but its distance from Viñales and the crags makes a car necessary on a daily basis.*

(each with a spectacular view and pool), but the distance from the crags likely necessitates a car. For most government-run hotels, including those in Viñales, knock one to two stars off the quality rating to reach an international standard – food and service are particularly poor. Because of this common complaint, most hotels now provide a buffet; at least you don't have to wait for the mediocre food.

Ecotourism Resorts

These hotels tend to be located near natural areas or out-of-the-way beaches, far from the chaos of Varadero and Havana. They often provide guided excursions such as hiking or snorkeling, but can be isolated and inundated with tour groups. Rancho San Vicente, seven kilometres from Viñales, falls into this category. There are also ecotourism resorts at Cayo Levisa and Maria La Gorda, beach areas of interest for climbers visiting Pinar del Río province.

FOOD & DRINK

Unless you find a *casa particular* with cooking facilities (there are none in Viñales), there will be few opportunities to prepare your own food in Cuba. These are the best dining options:

Private Rooms

If staying in a *casa particular*, your food problems will be solved as meals can be prepared daily by the family for a reasonable fee (breakfast $2–4 CUC and dinner $8–10 CUC). The food is generally tasty and plentiful. In Viñales, this is the only real option – there are no legal *paladares* and there is just a single, state-run restaurant and a few snack bars.

Government Restaurants

In general, restaurant dining in Cuba can be a frustrating experience. The state-run nature of the establishments often results in mediocre food and slow service, although there are exceptions – some restaurants and resort buffets have improved drastically due to past criticism. See page 29 for Havana recommendations.

Private Restaurants (*Paladares*)

For travellers, there is quality dining hope in the form of *paladares,* which are legally permitted, privately run, home-restaurants. They must employ family members only, are not supposed to serve lobster or beef, and are limited to 12 seats. They are restricted to certain areas, but almost every *paladar* has better service and food than the government restaurants. Entrées are typically under $10 CUC. See page 29 for Havana recommendations.

Groceries

Buying groceries in Viñales can be challenging, which is why it's best to eat at your *casa particular*. Viñales has a small grocery store, but the selection is limited and not well-suited to preparing your own meals. Good snack foods are not readily available

Cuban Cuisine *Visitors dine at the recommended state-run restaurant La Bodeguita in Havana (top) and getting ready to dive into a icy, sweet mojito at a beachside resort (left).*

either, so it's best to come prepared with a stock of energy bars and the like. Viñales has a small bakery (with restricted hours) for purchasing bread, and a farmer's market where it's possible to buy a selection of fruits and vegetables. Purchasing fruit while trudging around the local farms (like Raúl's) is also a viable option.

Bars

If you hope to take advantage of the cool, morning climbing conditions while in Viñales, resisting the temptations of the night will be one of your greatest challenges. There are three bars in town that feature nightly live music and, unlike the tourists clubs in Havana, are full of locals. Another option not to be missed is El Palenque, a bar by day and disco by night, located four kilometres north of town. The bar is inside a stalactite-riddled cave and provides a great aprés-climbing hangout with chilled beer and lush, frosty mojitos. The evening extravaganza is ever more exciting and features spectacularly clad dancers.

GETTING AROUND

For Cubans, transportation is one of the major hassles of daily life and the locals spend hours hitchhiking and waiting for buses, tractors or trucks. Luckily, for tourists with dollars, getting around the island is relatively easy.

Car Rentals

Car rentals in Cuba are easy, readily available, hassle-free and expensive, with prices ranging from $45–60 CUC per day for sub-compacts. The bus and taxi system is much cheaper and more than adequate for a climber visiting Cuba.

Taxis

In Havana, there are only a few taxi companies and the cars are metered, so there is no haggling over price. In Viñales, taxis congregate around the village square each morning. Since the price of a taxi ride is so much less than the cost of renting a car, this is a very good option for distant cliff transportation. A warning: return transportation may be unreliable, especially if your taxi is not from Viñales. Ask locals for a recommendation.

Buses

There are two bus lines that offer service between Havana and Viñales:

Víazul is a deluxe carrier; the terminal is in Nuevo Vedado, across from the zoo. Some Víazul buses, such as those to Viñales, can be booked and caught at the Havana Astro bus terminal, which is the most convenient. The Víazul buses are much nicer than the Astro buses and a ticket from Havana to Viñales is $12 CUC. Bring a sweater – the air conditioning is typically set on "high".

Astro is the national bus service and offers trips to Viñales. These buses are always full, hot and unreliable, but you don't need a reservation because dollar-paying tourists get priority. The Astro terminal in Havana is on Ave. Rancho Boyeros, e/ 19 de Mayo y Bruzón. A ticket to Viñales is $8 CUC.

Public Transportation

In Havana and other large cities, public transportation is available. Elsewhere, public transportation means bicycling, riding in a horse-drawn cart or hitchhiking in a car, truck or tractor.

Classic Automobiles *Cuba is rife with vintage American cars, left over from the 1950s when U.S. cars were still being imported into the country.*

VIÑALES

Viñales has remained a cozy, rural town of just a dozen streets or so. Despite its popularity with tourists, it has no large hotels, restaurants, or souvenir shops. People live in traditional tiled-roof homes in town or in Cuban *bohios* (huts) on the farms that are enveloped with rich red soil, perfect for growing tobacco. In addition to the town's moderate population, about 10,000 more people are scattered throughout the valley. Plows and carts are ox- or horse-drawn and the local farmers – *guajiros* – are seldom without a horse and machete. After a couple of days in town, you will feel at home and at ease finding your way around.

The approaches to climbs are through the farms and coffee groves. The *guajiros* have befriended the climbers, who give them old climbing ropes, which they use to tie up their oxen. In return, the farmers share their fruit and tobacco. If you think you can handle a *guajiro's* biting, rustic cigar, he will hand roll you a genuine Cuban "puro".

Finding Climbing Partners

It's easy to meet local and foreign climbers in Viñales because it's such a small town. Usually climbers spot each other. We are much more recognizable than we think and our clothing labels often give us away. If you are travelling solo, try staying at one of the *casas particulares* that climbers frequent and, if that fails, walk up to Cueva Cabeza de la Vaca in the afternoon and you will likely find visiting and local climbers scaling the shaded walls.

Viñales at a Glance...

Established:	1878
Elevation:	135 M
Population:	27 129
Time Zone:	EST
Phone Code:	48
To Havana:	188 KM
No. of *Casas*:	250+

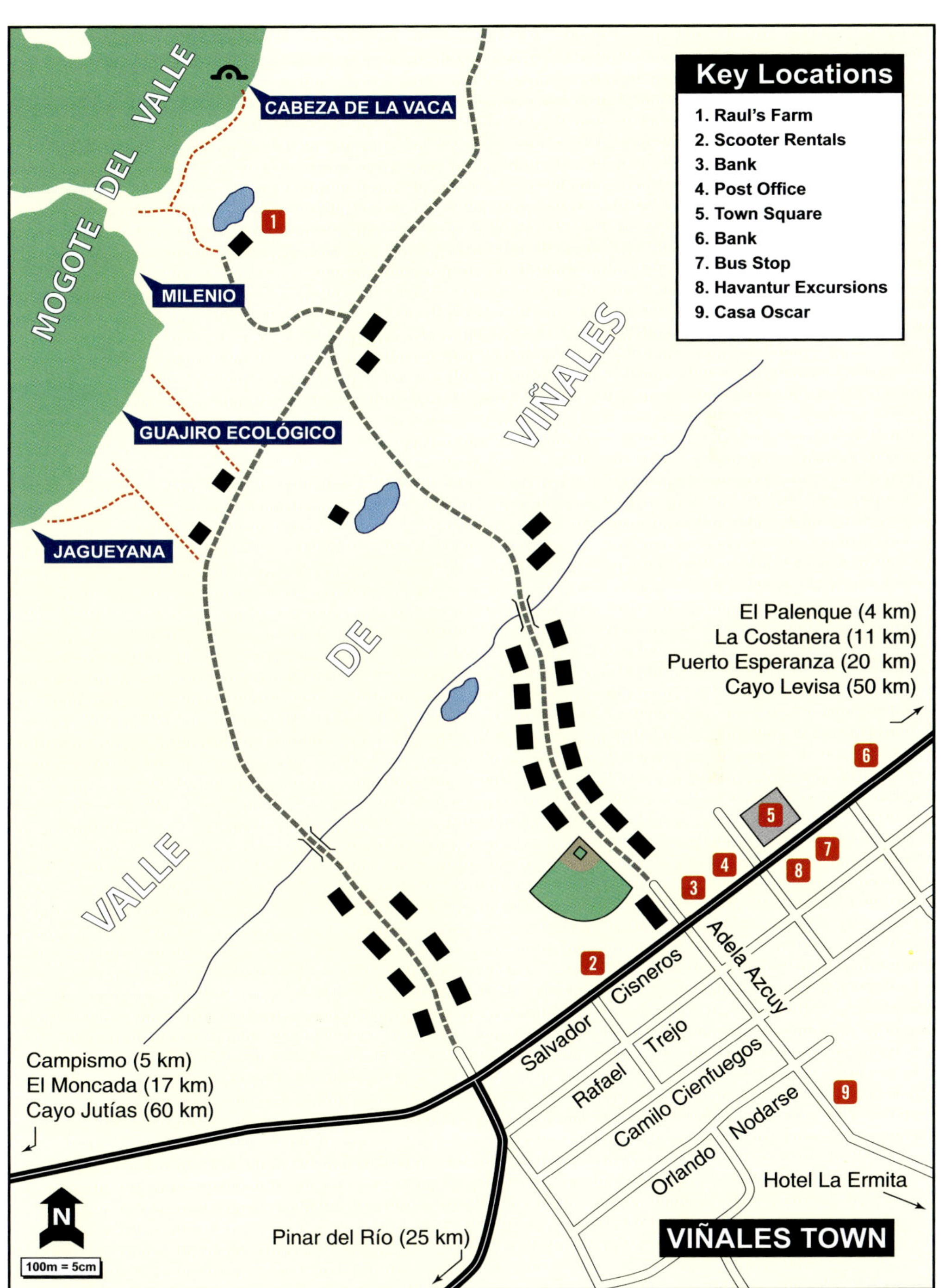

MOGOTE DEL VALLE
CABEZA DE LA VACA
1
MILENIO
GUAJIRO ECOLÓGICO
JAGUEYANA
VIÑALES
DE
VALLE
El Palenque (4 km)
La Costanera (11 km)
Puerto Esperanza (20 km)
Cayo Levisa (50 km)
6
5
4
7
8
3
2
9
Salvador
Cisneros
Trejo
Adela Azcuy
Rafael
Camilo Cienfuegos
Orlando
Nodarse
Hotel La Ermita
VIÑALES TOWN
Campismo (5 km)
El Moncada (17 km)
Cayo Jutías (60 km)
Pinar del Río (25 km)
N
100m = 5cm
Key Locations
1. Raul's Farm
2. Scooter Rentals
3. Bank
4. Post Office
5. Town Square
6. Bank
7. Bus Stop
8. Havantur Excursions
9. Casa Oscar

OTHER ACTIVITIES

One of the pleasures of visiting Viñales is the plethora of non-climbing activities available. Here are some recommendations to get you started:

Beaches

Cuba is a subtropical country with year-round swimming and the white-sand beaches are exquisite. The nicest beach close to Viñales is at Cayo Jutía. It is undeveloped and clean with an easy-to-swim-to-reef. There is a café/restaurant and a place to rent snorkelling gear. To get there, motorcycles and scooters are available to rent in Viñales with prices around $18 CUC per day. Alternatively, one of the taxis in Viñales will take you there and wait all day for about $35–40 CUC. Organize a group to reduce the per person cost.

Another good option, albeit a little farther away, is Cayo Levisa. This white-sand beach is accessed by boat and is very private and beautiful. Bus service from Viñales may be possible, but a taxi is more reliable.

For the adventurous, try Maria La Gorda on the western tip of the island, which is a destination snorkelling and diving site. It's at least a two-hour taxi ride from Viñales, but well worth the effort as the beach is beautiful and the water crystal clear with abundant sea life. Accommodation, food and snorkelling gear are all available.

Caving

The caving opportunities around Viñales are extensive. Gran Caverna de Santo Tomás, one of the largest caves with over 40 kilometres of tunnels, is only 15 kilometres from Viñales at Moncada. La Sociedad Espeleológica de Cuba has a "school" in Moncada and provides tours led by excellent guides. A good days' outing – by taxi, rented motorcycle or auto – is to explore the caves at Santo Tomás and then continue to Cayo Jutía.

Cockfights

Cockfighting is illegal in Cuba, but is often tolerated by local officials. Although the concept may be distasteful to some, it is an exhilarating cultural experience, not watching the birds fight, but watching the exuberance of the locals. Viñales is one place where, most Sundays, you can locate a cockfight. Ask around to find out where the "pelea" is. Locals are accustomed to foreigners being in attendance and rarely object to photography.

Hiking

Ecotourism is getting popular in Viñales and the national park offers guided hikes that can be arranged at Hotel La Ermita or in town through Havanatur Excursions. This is a great way to learn more about the local history, flora and fauna. If you prefer not to hire a guide, there is much hiking to be done on your own. The mogotes and sierras around Viñales have many valleys, caves and holes to explore. If you prefer not to walk, horses can easily be arranged – ask around. Alternatively, bikes are available to rent in town, but are expensive, perhaps $5 CUC per hour. Check with the owners of your *casa particular*; they may have bikes available.

Internet Access

For checking email, Internet service is periodically available in Viñales at a small telephone company office with computer terminals. The connection speeds vary, but tend to be on the slow side. Currently, there is no Wi-Fi in Viñales.

Viñales Botanical Garden

One site not on the tour bus circuit is the Viñales Botanical Garden. It is the personal work of two elderly widows and includes extensive varieties of trees, fruits, flowers and medicinal herbs. One of widows will personally give you a tour, although they do not speak English. It is at the north edge of town, across from the Cupet station.

HAZARDS & HEALTH

Food & Water

In general, the food in Cuba is very safe to eat as the level of hygiene and public health is high. Many visitors drink the local water without a problem, but if you want to play it safe, bottled water is readily available. Unfortunately, the plastic bottles are an environmental concern, so minimize their use when possible. Also, be sure to stay adequately hydrated, especially on the multi-pitch routes. Heat stroke has affected some climbers.

Disease

Although the environment around Viñales resembles the landscape of southern Thailand, there is a surprising lack of tropical diseases; malaria, typhoid and dysentery are absent. Immunizations should be unnecessary, but check with your doctor before you go.

Crime

Compared to many countries, Cuba is a very safe place to travel; mugging and theft are rare. However, do keep your valuables safe and if you rent a car, be careful with overnight parking. Car parts are scarce in Cuba and scrounging from rentals is very tempting.

Jineteros

Although not a hazard per se, Jineteros (hustlers) can be a serious annoyance to travellers. They will follow you around Havana, trying to sell you cigars, guide you to restaurants, etc. They are avoidable if you do not engage them in any way. Be polite, yet firm and *never* stop walking. Also, be careful of people offering to "guide" you to a *casa particular*, maybe even one that you've already booked. They will demand a commission from the owner, who will charge it back to you. Viñales is not immune.

Wasps

The major natural hazard to climbers in Viñales are wasps. Most climbing lines have been cleared, although wasps occasionally reclaim some territory. Usually, an active nest must be physically contacted to provoke an attack; simply climbing near it is usually safe. However, visitors with allergies must come fully prepared with epinephrine injection pens and/or antihistamines. Keep the medication in your climbing pack, if necessary.

Mosquitoes

Dengue fever, a mosquito-borne disease, has surfaced in Havana periodically over the past decade, but each time the government has responded aggressively and fumigated extensively. Regardless, good mosquito repellent is a strongly recommended addition to your pack due to the jungle-like environment surrounding some crags.

Poison Ivy

Cuban poison ivy (*guao*) is found around Viñales, but its range is not extensive.

Rappeling

One particular climbing hazard that deserves special mention is rappelling from over-hanging multi-pitch routes. These climbs almost always require special descending techniques with extra ropes to reach anchors located in overhangs and caves. There is a real possibility of being stranded in space if you make an error. If you are interested in experiencing these climbs and are inexperienced in these techniques, seek professional training before your trip and carry extra gear with you, such as prussik slings and ascenders.

Rescue

Currently, there is no organized high-angle rescue team in Viñales. If a problem did occur, the caving guides from Moncada have rescue training but, overall, it's best to come prepared with adequate personal gear and training. If a climber is injured, the best chance of a rescue will come from the other climbers at the cliff, and Cubans are never reluctant to help. If there is an accident, the victim will immediately be picked up, put into the nearest car, tractor, or cart and taken to a clinic or hospital.

Medicine & Hospitals

Some forms of medicine are hard to find in Cuba, so it's advisable to bring a good first aid kit. Viñales has an herbal pharmacy, a good polyclinic and many local doctors. In fact, if you get sick, do not be surprised if a doctor is immediately called to your casa – a genuine house call! The doctors are knowledgeable and you'll probably get a good diagnosis, but they are limited due to a lack of diagnostic equipment, x-rays and many pharmaceuticals. For a climber who has been injured, the closest major hospitals are in Pinar del Río, about 27 kilometres south of Viñales. One of the hospitals is on the north side of the city on Carretera Central, the main road that leads to Havana. Any local taxi driver should know the way. Cuba has a very high quality health care system for both locals and tourists and hospital emergency rooms are open around the clock. Carry insurance and be prepared to pay up front for treatments, although prices are far lower than in Western private hospitals and you will probably not be charged for local care.

Important Phone Numbers

Policlinico Fermin Valdez (Viñales)	phone: 793348
Abel Santamaria Hospital (Pinar del Río)	phone: 762068
Leon Cuervo Hospital (Pinar del Río)	phone: 754443
Emergency for Pinar del Río Province	phone: 762317

CLIMBING HISTORY

The Mystery of the Españolas:

The record of the first foreign climbers in Cuba is murky and was discovered long after the fact. In 1999, when Craig Luebben, Cameron Cross and Armando Menocal reached the top of the first pitch on the first ascent of the La Costanera "cathedral", they were surprised to discover three rusty pitons, a loop of perlon and a carabiner: an obvious rappel! A nearby *campesino* (farmer) told them that about 15–20 years ago, two Spanish women climbed for two days to reach that point on the wall. Apparently, the women went no farther, although Luebben thought he saw pin scars on the next pitch. The story of the Spanish climbers seemed dubious, but there was no denying that pitons were hammered long ago by someone. Although the identity of the climbers remain a mystery, the central section of cliff is named in their honour – La Bóveda de Las Españolas (The Celestial Vault of the Spanish Women).

The Early Cuban Climbers

Climbing in Cuba had a modest beginning. Slowly, a small group of Cubans in Havana began teaching themselves to climb using caving skills, meager caving gear, climbing magazines and a Petzl catalogue. Their initial approach to climbing fit their equipment and caving experience: drop in from above, drill an anchor and then toprope the route; the hangers were removed for reuse. A few of them were particularly anxious to move beyond the caving approach and these individuals became the first generation of true Cuban climbers: Vitalio (Vity) Echazábal, Jorge Mederos and Aníbal Fernández (who was only 13 at the time). With limited knowledge, equipment and experience, the scrappy Cubans managed to establish a few toprope routes at Jaruco, a limestone cliff about one hour east of Havana. More lasting, however, was the training ground they developed closer to home: the incut limestone walls of the Castle of the Three Holy Kings of El Morro. This castle is a landmark that has defined the entrance to Havana harbour for four centuries.

© CRAIG LUEBBEN

Around 1997, a toprope climbing competition was staged in the heartland of Cuba's limestone cliffs, the Viñales Valley. By then, the core of the Havana climbers included Echazábal, Fernández, Mederos, Carlos Pinelo, Humberto Abraham and Ananay Jiménez (who won the women's category). The Cubans were surprised by the size of the turnout at the competition; they were beginning to imagine that climbing could be a reality in their own country. Later that year, Alberto Morales, a climber/sports official from Colombia, attended a conference in Cuba. The Cubans took him to the Viñales Valley where they teamed up to establish the first route, a three-pitch gear climb they called *Colombia y El Caiman del Caribe* (three pitches, 6a) somewhere on the Mogote del Valle. Most importantly, though, was that when Morales went home, he left Echazábal his rack.

The Great Leap Forward

The next foreign climbers to visit Cuba were the catalysts that eventually launched Cuban climbing into the international spotlight. This was also the beginning of the gear donation tradition by foreign climbers that sustained and eventually installed the Cuban climbers as the leaders in new route exploration on their own land. In 1997 and 1998, two Americans with climbing roots in Wyoming, USA, separately visited the Viñales Valley in search of potential climbing. Skip Harper, who had climbed extensively at Vedauwoo and the Snowy Range, came to Cuba alone because he could find no one else to join him on the trip. The United States travel restrictions forced him to come in through the "back door" on an old DC-3 with no co-pilot and empty rivet holes in the walls – you could see the scenery outside! Harper was stunned to find a nearly uninhabited tropical climbing paradise.

In 1998, Armando Menocal, a long time climbing activist and mountain guide from Wyoming, returned to Cuba after a 40-year absence. Menocal's mother was born and raised in Cuba and, on his father's side, his great-grandmother's cousins included a former president, Mario Menocal García, and Cuba's famous classical painter, Armando Menocal, his namesake. Menocal returned to find his family roots and to check out a mountain region, Viñales, that the Lonely Planet guidebook described as a "miniature

Yosemite". Through the early morning mist, he saw Viñales' 1,000-foot, overhanging limestone walls, bulging with tufas and stalactites, rising above the lush green palms and dark red tobacco fields. It was a vast treasure of virgin rock. Menocal was so captivated with the region that he immediately planned a return trip, in February 1999, with a team of climbers from Colorado: climber Skip Harper, writer-photographer Craig Luebben and George Bracksieck, the founder of *Rock and Ice* magazine.

The Americans decided that they wanted not just to explore climbing in Cuba, but to climb with Cubans as well. Had others attempted to climb these wildly overhanging walls? Were there other climbers in Cuba? The Speleological Society proposed they put on a climbing presentation to see what kind of interest there was. Luebben had recently completed a touring slideshow in support of his just-published *ice* climbing book and set up a presentation at the sprawling Sports City campus in Havana. The broken window shades could not block the rays of the powerful tropical sun, making the images of ice climbing impossible to decipher, but the dozen Cuban climbers who attended did not seem to mind. The shared passion for climbing was infectious.

That afternoon, the Cubans took the visitors to climb at their local crag, the castle of El Morro. Its 50- to 60-foot walls of immense limestone blocks towered above the sea, providing an ideal and accessible climbing wall. The climbers shared the castle with sandlot baseball games, kids diving into the sea and cavers practicing rappelling. Local photographers posed Cuban girls in evening dresses next to the sea to chronicle their *quinceñeras* (their 15TH birthday and prelude to womanhood). As Menocal realized, "We weren't introducing the Cubans to climbing, they were showing us the resourceful, vibrant Cuban spirit." The next day, the Cubans took the Americans to their toprope area outside of Havana where Luebben bolted a 6b+, *Viva Cuba!*. Sport climbing in Cuba had officially begun.

Two of the Havana climbers at that first Sports City slideshow, Vity Echazábal and Carlos Pinelo, next joined the Americans in a month-long, rock exploration across Cuba culminating in an assault on the cliffs around Viñales. Vity, the most talented climber in the group, benefited greatly from the trip and was leading 6c routes in Viñales by the end – a huge leap forward in his ability! On the Americans' last day in Viñales, they were joined by another young Cuban with short, cropped blond hair. They did not know it at the time but Aníbal Fernández had gone AWOL from the army and hitchhiked to Viñales to climb with them and, after they dropped off Fernández back in Havana, he went straight to the brig for two weeks! But Aníbal Fernández was hooked and went on to develop many routes in Viñales. He was also likely Cuba's first climbing celebrity and appeared on a big, eye-catching poster advertising cigarettes.

Later, the Havana climbers seduced another strong and extremely committed climber, Abel Pérez, a student of industrial design. He climbed and bouldered throughout the summer, but when school resumed in the fall, he found himself in class thinking only of climbing. He dropped out, despite the vehement objection of his father, and returned to Viñales. Ardent, quiet and focused, Abel discovered that he wanted only to climb, and mostly on new routes. "My father thinks that climbing is stupid. Cuba has no culture of climbing," Abel explained. In time, he became the second Cuban to climb 8a.

The first routes done in Viñales were not by Americans alone, but always with the help of the neophyte Cubans. From the beginning, the Americans brought gear, which quickly developed into a full-fledged donation program supported by a dozen climbing companies. In Cuba, route exploration and development necessitated power drills and bolts. One bolt and hanger would cost only slightly less than a month's salary for a Cuban; an entire route, a years' pay. Saving for a Bosch or Hilti drill could take a lifetime. Menocal brought a couple of used power drills for the Cubans to use and later, Canadian Paul Laperrière donated a new 36-volt Hilti! This empowered the Cubans to start developing their own crags, a practice rarely seen in a third-world country.

Josué Millo

© BETH WALD

Filling in the Gaps

By the end of 1999, the first year of exploration, most of the large faces on the valley's mogotes had at least one route. From his first visit, Craig Luebben demonstrated an eye and ardour for the biggest walls, which earned him the nickname, "Mr. Mogote". On his initial expedition, he did the dramatic classic *Cuba Libre* (three pitches, 7a+), the quintessential Cuban route – steep and heavily featured. Then, teaming up with Cameron Cross, Luebben did the longest climbs in Cuba, the five-pitch routes *Mr. Mogote* (7a+) and *Flyin' Hyena* (7b), the latter being the direct route up the centre of *La Bóveda de Las Españolas*. Luebben and Cross finished off their season with an enchainment of these three routes in a day.

In 2000, Luebben and Cross returned to add another three long, hard routes at La Costanera, including the ultra-dubious *Have a Cigar* (7c). David Ryan, an Exum Guide from Wyoming, also established several potential five-star routes including *Colmillo Blanco* (two pitches, 6a), *Filo de Cuchilla* (two pitches, 6a+) and the spectacular, overhanging *Mucho Pumpito* (two pitches, 6b), which has become a "must-do" for visiting climbers.

2001 saw Cuban climbers take the lead with Vity Echazábal and Aníbal Fernández putting up two long, difficult routes: *Milenio*, (three pitches, 6c+) and *Huevos Verde con Jamon* (two pitches, 6c+). Echazábal also opened the futuristic, tufa-laced Ancón Wall, with *Alimentando Mosquitos* (6b+). To this day, Ancón is still grossly underdeveloped. During this

same season, teams of Cubans and Americans returned to La Costanera, the cliff that has yielded, by far, the most multi-pitch routes in Cuba. Fernández and Ryan climbed the inside corner on the right side of the wall to complete *Chicken Run* (four pitches, 7a+) and Echazábal added *Viernes 13* (four pitches, 7a).

Around the same time, Pinelo, Ryan and Cuban-American Fernando Paulette, suffered through bat scat, poison oak and thorns on Mileno Wall to create the 3-pitch *Guao, Guano, y Espina* (6b), which is one of the most popular climbs of the grade. Several groups of notable visiting climbers also raised standards of difficulty. Spaniard David Brasco put up an amazing 18 routes in May 2001, developing the entire Guajiro Ecológico Wall. He also opened a route that has become *the* testpiece for neophyte Cuban climbers, *Malanga Hasta La Muerte* (7b+) at Cueva Cabeza de la Vaca.

Spring 2002 saw the arrival of a team of six talented British climbers, travelling the world in search of perfect new routes. The Brits contributed perspective to the local scene and es-

© MIKE ROBERTSON

tablished Cuba's hardest route to date, Tim Emmett's *The One Inch Punch* (8b+). In one month, the team added many routes, including Neil Gresham's and Mike Robertson's *The Wasp Factory* (7b+), which has become a climb against which visitors measure their likely success on Cuba's cliffs. The team also climbed seven new routes on the overhangs and stalactites of Cuba Libre Wall, including Charlie Woodburn's *The Rum Diaries*, (7b+), which, as Charlie put it, "gives *Cuba Libre* what it might have been looking for – a direct start and wicked, sustained moves for the grade!" Finally, Gresham invented a free start to the implausibly acrobatic *Have a Cigar* (8a) and Sheffield grit master, Seb Grieve, summed it up by claiming, "If that climb we did today was at any of the top climbing areas of the world, it would be among the absolute best, without a doubt."

In time, the distinguishing characteristics of the mogotes of the Valle de Viñales may be their multi-pitch routes. There are now more than two dozen of these classic routes on the valley's big walls, which require endurance to climb and technical descending skills to escape.

The Present

Today, Cubans dedicated to climbing full-time live in Viñales, a genuine sign of the popularity and quality of this climbing region. The most prolific of these climbers and the ones currently mentoring the next generation include Alberto Leivas, Reinel Sosa, Jorge "El Gato" Luis, Raikel Reyes and Yarobys García. García was the first Cuban to onsight 7c and Leivas, in his own quiet way, has become the strongest climber in Cuba today. He was the first to climb 8a and, later, 8b+, when he made the second ascent of Emmett's *One Inch Punch*. However, the first and, by far, most prolific of these home-grown Viñales climbers was Josué Millo. His tenure overlapped with Aníbal Fernández, and from 2002 through 2005, the two Cubans led development of new routes and together totally dominated climbing in the Viñales Valley.

Many of the first generation of Cuban climbers have now emigrated from Cuba. Carlos Pinelo and Aníbal Fernández came to Wyoming for a rock guide course in 2001. Pinelo dropped out midway through and defected, but Fernández took full advantage of the course and climbed both El Cap and Half Dome, returning to Cuba afterward. That same year, Vity Echazábal, Jorge Mederos and Ananay Jiménez, on a training program to Spain, also chose to stay. Abel Pérez, the young student who had dropped out of school so he could put up routes, left Cuba in 2006. Aníbal Fernández eventually left Cuba in 2005, and two years later, so did Josué Millo. They trained, mentored and equipped the next generation of climbers and their legacy may not be measured in the routes they established, but in the creation of the present Cuban community of climbers.

In Viñales, a new group of men and women are now climbing almost daily. The newcomers include young, fit farmers, testing themselves on the many difficult climbs when not working in the fields. Most days you can find some of them training on *Malanga Hasta La Muerte* or on the nearby route *The Wasp Factory*, the benchmarks of skill and strength for the new climbers. Since Alberto Leivas' recent departure for Barcelona, the unquestioned leader today is Yarobys García. He is an exceptional climber and is committed to the challenge of opening new routes and mentoring the next generation.

Tobacco *Cuban cigars are famous and Pinar del Río account for about 59% of the country's plantations. Here, a farmer inspects leaves in a secadero — a special curing barn oriented to catch maximum sunlight. The leaves are sewn together in pairs and hung over wooden poles to dry for about 50 days.*

HOW TO USE THIS BOOK

The cliffs described in this book are generally ordered from west to east – the layout of the climbing region is shown on an overview map on the inside cover. There are seven climbing chapters in this book and each includes a general description of the area along with an overview map to show the position of the crags. Each crag contains an introduction and a description of the character of the climbing, along with details of the approach.

Cliff Icons

Each cliff page in the book has a bar across the top containing a number of icons. The intent is to provide an overview of the nature of the crag, which should help in choosing an appropriate venue. Refer to the icon list on the opposite page for specific explanations.

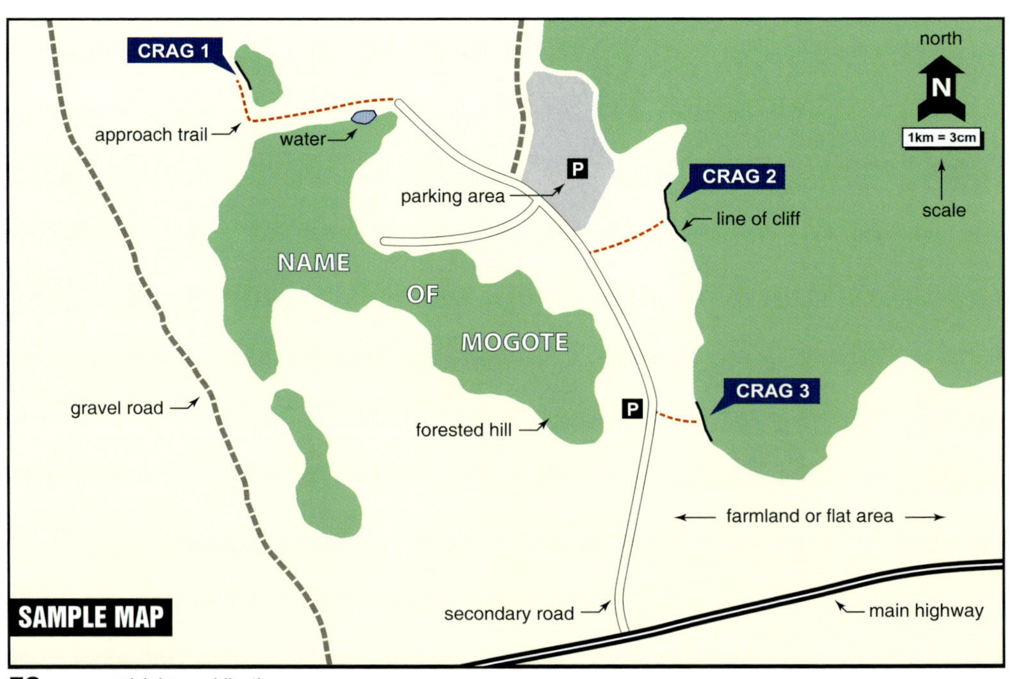

Maps

The overview and approach maps in this book are standard topographical style, providing a "top down" view of the area in question. See the sample map on the opposite page for specific features.

Cliff Photos

Most routes in the book are represented on a photograph. A red line shows the approximate path of the climb along with the location of the anchor. See the sample photo below for more information.

Route Descriptions

All climbing routes in the book are numbered – **blue** climbs are fully bolted and **red** climbs require gear. French grades are used to rate the climbs and a conversion chart is included on the back cover flap. Red stars rate quality, a "tick box" is provided for tracking your climbs and first ascent details come at the end.

Icon Key

☐	Tick box
★	Poor
★★	Average
★★★	Good
★★★★	Very good
★★★★★	Excellent
	Drive to crag
	Hiking time
	Sun all day
	Morning sun
	Afternoon sun
	No sun
	Low-angle
	Vertical
	Overhanging
	Windy
	May seep
	Dry in rain

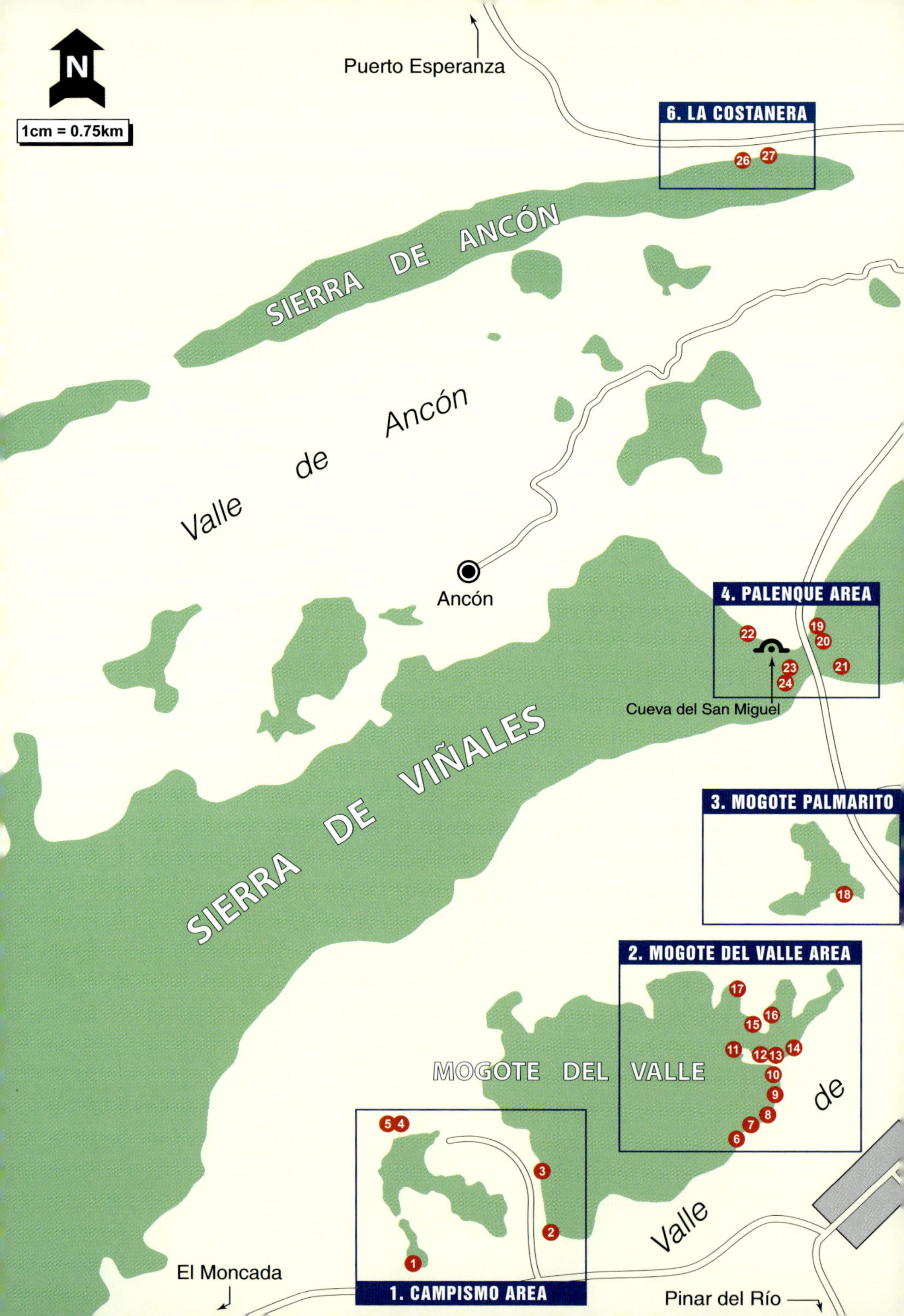

N
1cm = 0.75km
Puerto Esperanza
6. LA COSTANERA
26 27
SIERRA DE ANCÓN
Valle de Ancón
Ancón
4. PALENQUE AREA
22
19
20
23
24
21
Cueva del San Miguel
3. MOGOTE PALMARITO
18
SIERRA DE VIÑALES
2. MOGOTE DEL VALLE AREA
17
15 16
11 12 13 14
10
9
8
7
6
MOGOTE DEL VALLE
de
El Moncada
5 4
3
2
1
Valle
1. CAMPISMO AREA
Pinar del Río

1. Mogote Santero
2. Esquina Caliente
3. Pared Campismo
4. Esquina Aníbal
5. Esquina Festival
6. Jagueyana
7. Cueva Larga
8. Guajiro Ecológico
9. Los Tormentos
10. Milenio
11. Ensenada de Raúl
12. Filo de Cuchilla
13. Torre Menoco
14. Cabeza de la Vaca
15. Paredón de Josué
16. Jaruquiño
17. Sector Geisha
18. Mogote Palmarito
19. Palenque Wall
20. Ferocity Wall
21. Mr. Mogote Wall
22. Cueva de San Miguel
23. Cuba Libre Wall
24. Paraíso Escondido
25. Mogote de los Hoyos
26. La Bóveda de las Españolas
27. Pared Silvía

CAMPISMO AREA

This large and varied zone is comprised of the crags surrounding the Campismo dos Hermanas on the west end of Mogote del Valle. The Campismo has small cottages and a swimming pool, which makes it a convenient après-climbing hangout, but to lodge there requires transportation as it's about five kilometres from the town of Viñales.

This area was the site of the first completed route in Viñales and has since expanded into a recommended multi-sector climbing area. There are numerous crags scattered throughout this region that provide various aspects and climbing styles, including the longest route on the Mogote del Valle. While in the area, check out the bizarre Mural de la Prehistoria and have lunch at the restaurant — the food is tasty!

© ANDREW BURR (VIÑALES STONEHENGE)

CAMPISMO AREA APPROACH

You could walk to this area with enough determination and time, but driving (or hitch-hiking) is recommended due to the distance from town. To get to Campismo dos Hermanas, take the main road west from Viñales toward El Moncada for about three kilometres and watch for signs for Mural de la Prehistoria and Campismo dos Hermanas. Once at this intersection, continue straight ahead to reach Mogote Santero or turn right off the main road and drive about two kilometres to reach Campismo dos Hermanas and all the other crags.

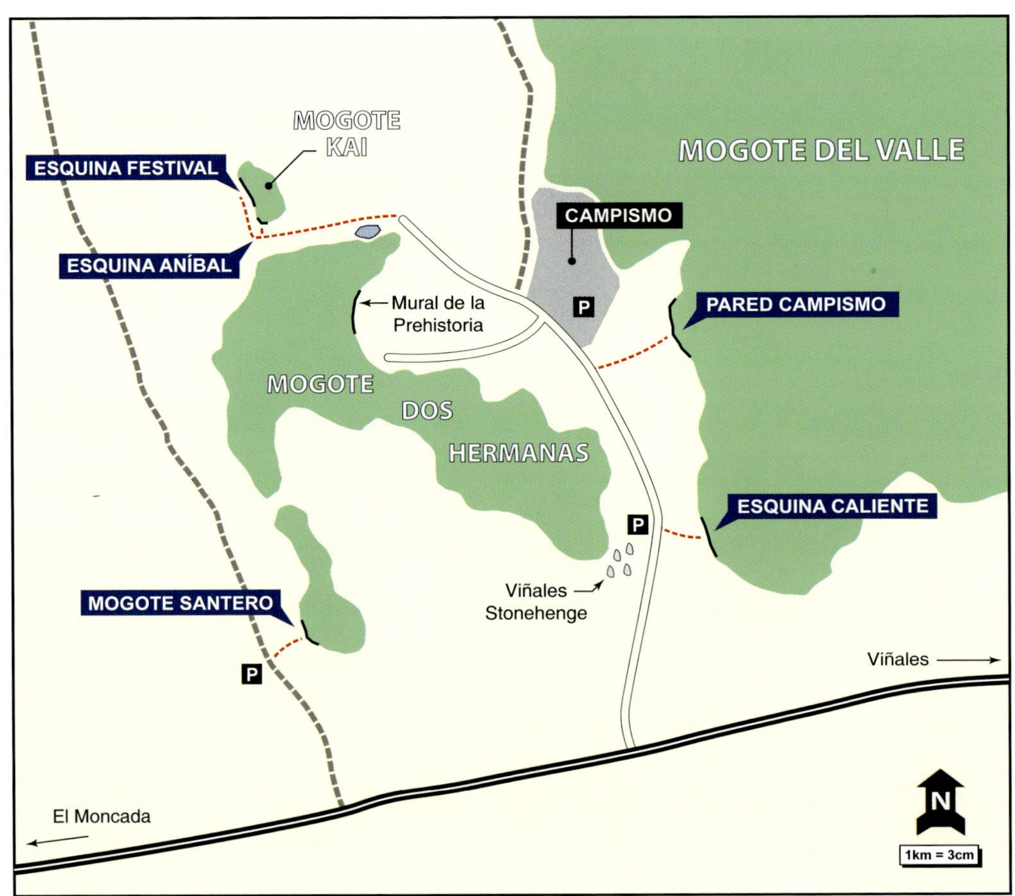

Campismo Dos Hermanas *The Campismo offers visitors cabin rentals at very reasonable rates and includes a restaurant and swimming pool. Local activities include horseback riding, rock climbing, caving, hiking and an archeological museum.*

Mural de la Prehistoria *Opinions may vary on the artistic merit of this mural, but it's a local landmark worth visiting. The painting was created in 1961 and the characters are meant to depict the process of evolution.*

Endless Rock *Looking west down the road to El Moncada. All the stone in the background is unexplored.*

MOGOTE SANTERO

Mogote Santero is the most westerly of the developed cliffs around Viñales and the routes are fairly recent additions. It has a beautiful 70-metre red wall that faces northwest, so it stays shaded until late afternoon. The base is quite steep and some scrambling is required to reach the climbs. Currently, there are no fixed ropes to help with this approach, but that may change in the near future.

APPROACH

Drive west out of Viñales toward Campismo Dos Hermanas and Moncada. After about three kilometres, the mogote starts to come into view near the turnoff for the Campismo. Initially, it appears completely covered with vegetation, but the clean, developed face is on the opposite side. To find it, continue driving down the main road, passing the turn-off for the Campismo, until you can see the climbable northwest face. Look for a dirt road and turn right, following it for 250 metres to a *bodega* (small farmer's convenience store). Park here. Cross fields to the base of the talus and then look for a trail marked with tape on the trees that leads up to the wall. Total walking time is approximately 10 minutes.

THE CLIMBING

This wall lacks the giant tufas and stalactites found on the other cliffs in the area, but it's still significantly steep and underdeveloped. The cliff has three distinctive bulges and the climbs predominantly utilize edges, cracks, huecos and flakes. Overall, the rock is sound, except for a small patch of friable conglomerate along the base.

Mogote Santero

Routes are listed from right to left.

❶ Insomnio 7b ★★★★★ . . . . ☐

This line follows the right edge of the wall and starts at the lowest end of the base. The first two pitches can be linked with 18 quickdraws. Bring a second rope for the rappel.

pitch 1 (6c, 28 m) Climb the grey wall.
pitch 2 (6b+, 8 m) Angle to the left.
pitch 3 (7b, 25 m) Finish through the overhangs. Bring 11 quickdraws.
3 pitches, bolts *FA: Yarobys García & Alberto Javier Leivas, 2006.*

❷ Miel para Ochún 7b ★★★★ . . . . ☐

The route is great, but a bees' nest close to the start will discourage some.
1 pitch (25 m), 10 bolts *FA: Yarobys García & Alberto Javier Leivas, 2006.*

❸ Sala Malecu 7a+ ★★★★ . . . . ☐

To reach the start, walk around the big boulder and up to a ledge (a rope *should* be placed to facilitate this). This is a future classic that requires a combination of techniques. It finishes on the ledge.
1 pitch (25 m), 10 bolts *FA: Alberto Javier Leivas & Yarobys García, 2006.*

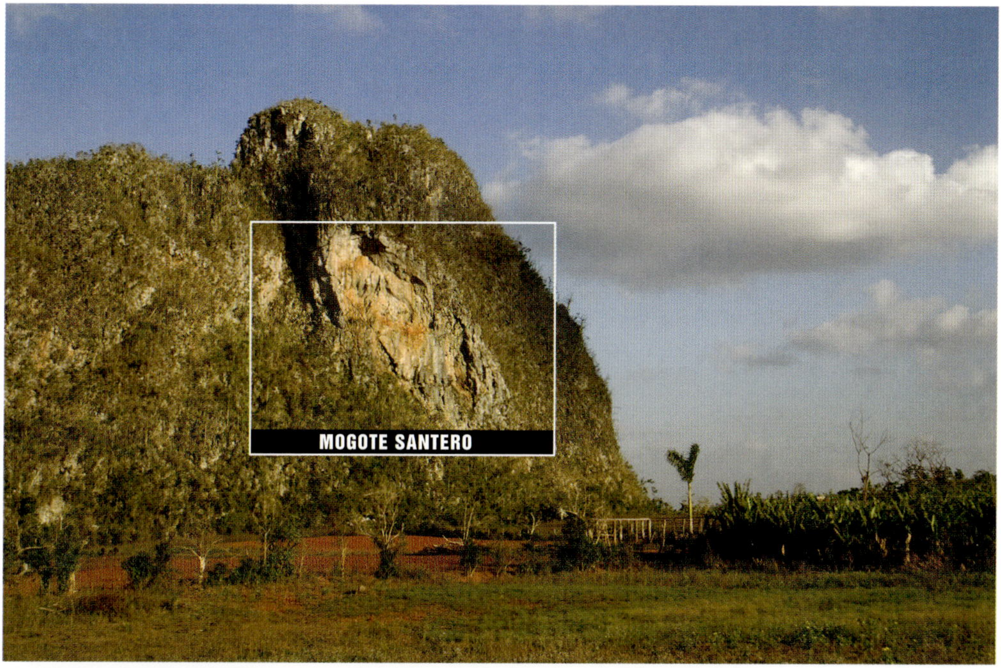

MOGOTE SANTERO

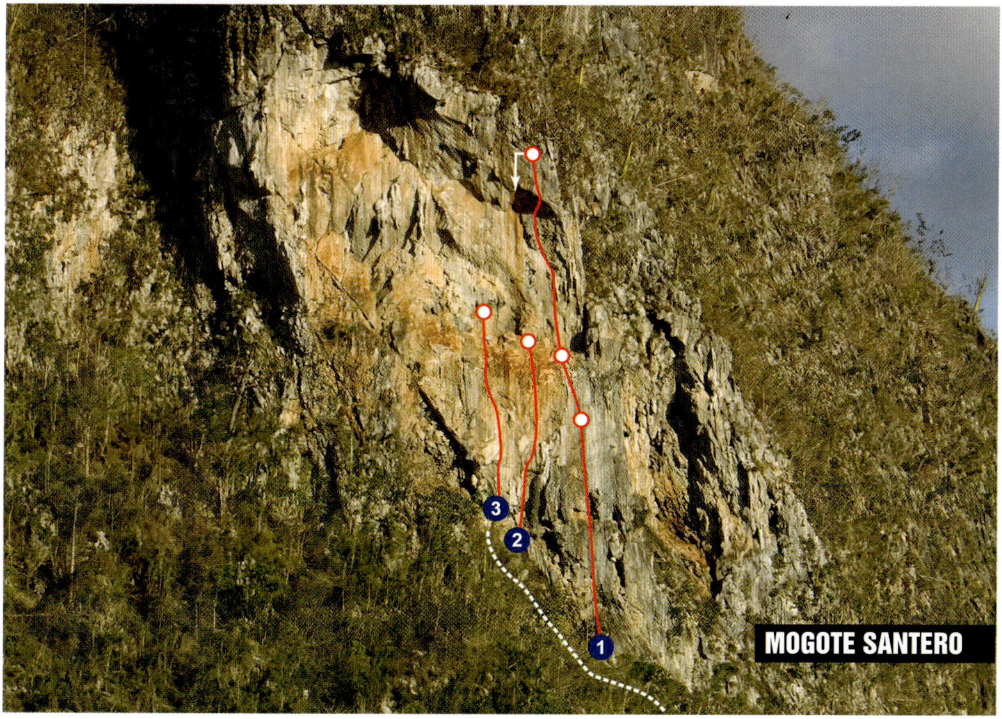

MOGOTE SANTERO

ESQUINA CALIENTE

Esquina Caliente – Hot Corner – is a nice, little crag that sits at the south-to-west bend of the massive Mogote del Valle. It's the first cliff encountered after turning off the main road toward Campismo Dos Hermanas and has a brief approach. There are a few nice moderates here and one tricky testpiece, making the crag well worth a half-day visit.

APPROACH

Drive west out of Viñales and, after about three kilometres, take the right-hand turnoff to Campismo Dos Hermanas. Follow this road until the cliff becomes apparent on the right side of the road. The routes are across a cultivated field behind a big Jaguey tree. Park on the shoulder and pick up the obvious trail to the crag, a five-minute walk.

THE CLIMBING

The cliff has a few nice moderates and a technical 7c testpiece to play on. The routes are located on both the steep pillar with the ficus tree to the right and the low-angle wall to the left. There is a big chimney here for reference.

Esquina Caliente

Routes are listed from right to left.

❶ Tarzán 6a+ ★ . . . . ☐

This obscure, perhaps unrepeated route, is on a small grey wall hidden behind trees to the right. Start on the roots of the Jaguay tree at the base, directly under the arête, and then climb the crack up and right. Bring medium size stoppers and camming devices.
1 pitch (30 M), gear *FA: Aníbal Fernández, 2002.*

❷ Titanic 6c ★★★★ . . . . ☐

This is the first bolted line that climbs straight up the face left of the ficus roots.
1 pitch (30 M), bolts *FA: Aníbal Fernández & Josué Millo, 2002.*

❸ Naufragio 6c ★★★ . . . . ☐

Use the first two bolts of *Titanic* and then go left instead of up.
1 pitch (20 M), bolts *FA: Aníbal Fernández & Alexei Suárez, 2003.*

❹ Madam Gruchenca 7c ★★★★★ . . . ☐

This route is farther left. Start almost inside the wide chimney and then climb the slightly overhanging face. This is a popular testpiece for the locals that features technical moves on small holds. It's always in the shade.
1 pitch (20 M), bolts *FA: Aníbal Fernández & Alexei Suares, 2003.*

❺ Pilar 6a+ ★★★ . . . . ☐

Climb the low angle pillar left of the wide crack.
1 pitch (28 M), bolts *FA: Aníbal Fernández & Abel Pérez, 2003.*

❻ Sibaricú 5+ ★★ . . . . ☐

Climb the dirty chimney left of the pillar. Not recommended.
1 pitch (25 M), bolts *FA: Aníbal Fernández & Abel Pérez, 2003.*

YAROBYS GARCÍA

PARED CAMPISMO

This red wall is to the right of the road across cultivated fields and is encountered just before reaching the Campismo. The best landmark may be the clean band of rock that is the long line of *Cuenta con la Pelóna*.

APPROACH

From Viñales, drive to the Campismo Dos Hermanas and park. Walk back down the approach road and pick up the trail that leads across the fields to the crag.

THE CLIMBING

The highlight of this cliff is the quality multi-pitch climb, *Cuenta con la Pelóna*.

Pared Campismo

Routes are listed from left to right.

❶ Pantalones Apretados 5 ★★★ ....☐

This is a short, easy climb on the far left side of the grey face.
1 pitch (15 M), bolts *FA: Josué Millo, 2003.*

❷ Vaca y Pollito 5+ ★★★ ....☐

This climb is slightly harder than *Pantalones Apretados*. Start up the edge of a small overhang; this section seeps and is often wet.
1 pitch (15 M), bolts *FA: Josué Millo & Alberto Javier Leivas, 2003.*

❸ Cuenta con la Pelóna 6b ★★★★★ ☐

This is a classic for the grade. Try it late in the afternoon or on a cool, cloudy day since it gets a good amount of sun. The climb starts right of the cave and big trees; the clean band of rock marks the route's path.

pitch 1–4 (5, 5, 6b, 6b) Climb the grey wall in four pitches. Trend left, always following the cleaned rock. The crux pitch goes directly up an orange face to finish under the jungle.
Descent: Bring at least two 50 m ropes to rappel. Some moderate pendulums are required.
4 pitches, bolts *FA: J. Millo & R. Sosa, 2003.*

❹ ¿Y Tu de que Te Ries? 7a ★★★★★ ☐

This route starts at the base of an obvious chimney inside a forest and climbs a challenging yellow face. It is over 35 metres long, so either lower carefully and downclimb the bottom section or bring a second rope.
1 pitch (35 M), bolts *FA: Alberto Leivas, Josué Millo & Jessy Gómez, 2005.*

❺ Makandal 6a+ ★★★★ ....☐

This route starts at the base of the chimney, as for *¿Y tu de que te Ries?*, but takes an easier line on the right. It is a nice moderate climb that is often shaded and climbs a natural line. Use the same descent technique as before.
1 pitch (35 M), bolts *FA: Aníbal Fernández, 2002.*

❻ Colombia y el Caimán del Caribe 6a ....☐

The exact location of this route is unknown because it was the first completed climb in the valley. All that is know is that it is somewhere to the right. It is said to have a jungle-like feel and no anchors were placed. Somewhere up in the trees and Drago Palms is a piece of rappel webbing marking the high point.
3 pitches, gear *FA: Alberto Morales, Vitalio Echazábal & Robertico.*

1
2
3
4
5
6
PARED CAMPISMO

ESQUINA ANÍBAL

This little crag is located on the diminutive Mogote Kai, which is a bit off the beaten path. It's north of the Dos Hermanas mogote and on the other side of its unique painted wall – the Mural de la Prehistoria. This mogote was discovered by the first foreign climber to come to Cuba solely to boulder, Kai Staats of Colorado, USA. Consequently, there is some fun bouldering at the base!

APPROACH

Drive west out of Viñales and, after three kilometres, take the right-hand turnoff to Campismo Dos Hermanas. Follow this road to the Campismo and park. The trail to the cliff starts just left of the Campismo gate. Follow the trail as it curves to the left, eventually travelling through the narrow corridor between Mogote Dos Hermanas and Mogote Kai. The wall becomes visible on the right, about 20 minutes from the parking area.

THE CLIMBING

There are no moderates at this steep crag. It's best to combine a visit here with a couple of the other cliffs in the area, or the nearby Esquina Festival.

Tocororo *The Cuban Trogon (Priotelus temnurus) is a species of bird in the Trogonidae family. Also known as the Tocoloro, it is endemic to and the national bird of Cuba. Its natural habitats are dry forests, moist lowland forests and moist mountain forests in the tropics and subtropics. It may also be found dwelling in heavily degraded former forests.*

Esquina Aníbal

Routes are listed from left to right.

① Nuestra Historia 7a ★★★ .... ☐

This route is farthest left and climbs to the obvious stalactites up high.

1 pitch (15 M), bolts *FA: Ned Harris.*

② Recuérdo 8a ★★★★ .... ☐

This hard route starts off the obvious boulder. The crux is at the very bottom so get an attentive belay to avoid decking.

1 pitch (17 M), bolts *FA: Tom Zappe & Aníbal Fernández, 2004.*

③ El Hombre, la Hembra y el Hambre 7b ★★★★★ ..... ☐

This route also starts on top of the boulder, but farther right than *Recuerdo*. It features long moves that link good features.

1 pitch (17 M), bolts *FA: Aníbal Fernadez, 2004.*

ESQUINA FESTIVAL

Like Esquina Aníbal, this cliff is also located on the small Mogote Kai (see photo on previous page). The locals organized an informal competition here, hence the "festive" name.

APPROACH

Approach as for Esquina Aníbal. Upon reaching that crag, turn left and follow the base of the mogote northward to find this little crag hidden behind the trees. This cliff is about a 25-minute walk from the parking area.

THE CLIMBING

There are two steep climbs here that are worth checking out. They make a good compliment to the harder routes at Esquina Aníbal. There is a lot of nice stone on this cliff that has not yet been developed.

Esquina Festival

Routes are listed from left to right.

❶ Deja que Te Coja 6b+ ★★★ . . . . ☐
The route on the left.
1 pitch, (15 M) 7 bolts *FA: Yarobys García & José Porras, 2006.*

❷ Chicos, no lloren 6c+ ★★★ . . . . ☐
The route on the right. This was the final climb of the competition in 2006.
1 pitch (10 M), 6 bolts *FA: Yarobys García & José Porras, 2006.*

Memories of Cuba don't cohere into a tidy tale when I conjure them. That's not to say Cuba doesn't remain vivid in my mind: how can a climber forget the death-squeal of a 300-pound pig, heard while walking off to the quiet crags in the Caribbean heat; or a giant birthday cake on the flatbed trailer of a horse-drawn cart, bound for a Sweet-16th, seen during the tired stroll back into town after hours on overhanging limestone. But the memories are so vivid they don't encourage narrative; they encourage only description. Sitting on a warm belay ledge, for example, in the sunshine, looking over tiny tobacco plots lain crazy-quilt-style over the reddish earth, smoke tendrils rising from thatched farm houses, and the town a little beyond, where we'd buy a lousy dinner that night, and sleep in a simple bed.

Men plow fields with oxen in Cuba; right underneath you, while you climb, they whip the big beasts up and down the crop rows. Wizened farmers, as you walk the dirt path back from yet another day's cragging, can sell you bananas and mangoes, but they can also sell you hand-rolled cigars from their own fields. You don't have to be a smoker to enjoy one of the world's rare treats and come to understand the fuss about Cuban tobacco. Nor do you have to be an alcoholic or a baseball fan to savor an afternoon of cigars, local rum and nine innings between Jose Contreras' old team, the Pinar Del Río Vegueros, and the Viñales boys. Sitting in the shaded concrete bleachers, the paint job perhaps twenty years old, and the grassy outfield untended, and the one plastic batting helmet passing between teams for each at-bat. You just have to be a human being, open to experience, aware that you're slipping into a one-of-a-kind culture with a real understanding of what makes life worthwhile.

The routes are ridiculous: wildly overhung, and with so many big, positive pockets and weirdo stalactites that even the unfit can find ways to hang on. And here's the oddest thing of all: while Cuba is crushingly poor (and communist, and tropical, and trapped in a dark totalitarian night), climbing does not feel out of place there. It does not feel out of place because Cubans do appear at the cliffs, with odd-ball collections of donated climbing gear, and they climb ferociously and well. And it does not feel out of place because of the texture of Cuban culture: countless well-attended amateur boxing matches; feverish betting on bloody cockfights; old American cars kept not just running but fantastically restored, like ongoing performance art projects; more live music than you've ever heard in your life, pumping out of every bar in every piss-ant town; salsa dancing so hot and fast and fine that you'll want to do like I did and hire a local for some lessons, just to get that vibe. Climbing doesn't feel out of place in Cuba, in other words, because Cuban culture is powerfully suffused with style, and grace, and the hunger for self-expression, and the irrepressible will to live a life less ordinary, no matter the circumstances.

Daniel Duane - San Francisco, California, 2009

CHAPTER 2

MOGOTE DEL VALLE

The striking Mogote del Valle is the large, jungle-shrouded pincushion hill that rises above the farms just northwest of the village of Viñales. The topography of this lush mogote is particularly conducive to rock climbing as the steep hillsides contain many exposed limestone walls and undercut caves.

Due to its proximity to town, the Mogote del Valle has always been the focus of local climbing efforts and now has the greatest concentration of developed cliffs in the region. The many sectors described in this chapter provide a plethora of climbing styles and grades, enough to keep most climbers busy for weeks. If you travel to Cuba to climb and choose not to rent a car, fear not as every cliff in this section is easily approachable on foot.

MOGOTE DEL VALLE APPROACH

All of the crags in this zone are approached on foot from downtown Viñales (see map page 39). To start, find Salvador Cisneros, the main road that runs through the village. From this street, there are two options to access the Mogote del Valle crags. The first takes a small road, one block west of the town square, that goes by the baseball field. Follow this ever-narrowing track to Raúl's farm, the access point for all the crags adjacent to the fields including those on the other side of the Cabeza de la Vaca tunnel. The second approach option takes a parallel road, one block west of the baseball field. Follow this track to some farms located in front of the obvious, orange-streaked Guajiro Ecológico wall. Use this option to access any of the cliffs adjacent to that sector.

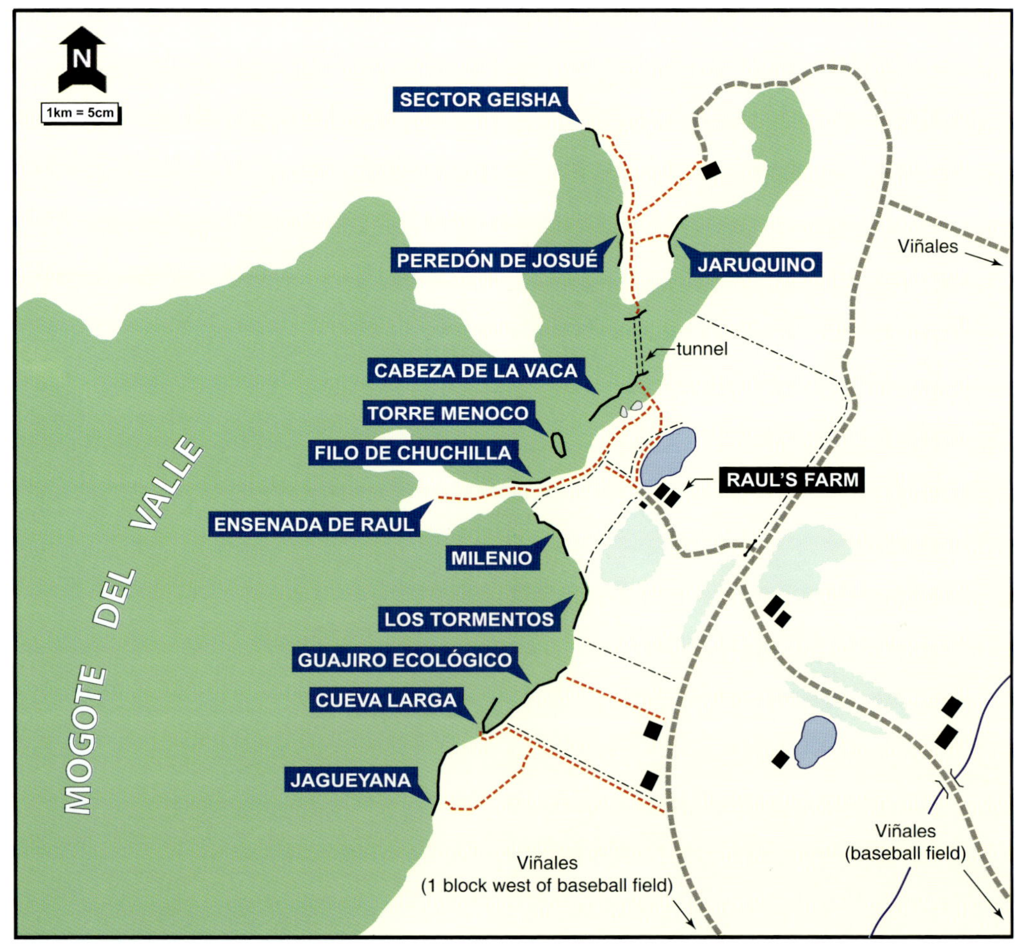

Tropical Fruit *Most of the excellent crags in this zone are accessed through the farm of Raúl Reyes. Raúl has shown great enthusiasm toward the climbers that visit this area and he graciously allows them to cross his fields. He sells locally grown fruit to passersby from a stand by his small house.*

Casual Approaches *Walking toward the Mogote del Valle crags, a pleasant 20-minute stroll from town. Los Tormentos and Milenio are the cliffs visible above the white house.*

JAGUEYANA

Jagueyana is a popular little crag that sports twenty enjoyable rock climbs. This cliff offers a diversity of climbing, a veil of shade and one of the shortest approaches from town. The cliff was discovered during a hot April in 2002 by local Cuban climbers looking for a shady wall close to town; development started immediately. The shade is welcome, but remember the template of the tropics: screening the sun often diverts the wind, which can garner mosquitoes.

APPROACH:

The small cliff of Jagueyana is located about 100 metres left of La Yunta. It is partially hidden by trees, mainly a big Jaguey *(Ficus stahlii)*, which both characterizes and names the crag. When approaching, the most noticeable feature from the trail is a dihedral with an overhanging left wall. This cliff is about a 20-minute walk from Viñales. Note that farmers often tie their cows close to this cliff: it's best to keep your distance.

THE CLIMBING:

Jagueyana offers a diversity of high quality single pitch routes at moderate grades. Here you'll find short bouldery lines with scary monos, jug-blessed overhangs, painful cracks and sustained arêtes. The climbs here are all bolt protected and range in length from 15–30 metres. The cliff receives shade all day except for the climbs on the extreme left end.

Jagueyana

Routes are listed from right to left.

① Miseria Prieta 7b+ ★★★ .... ☐

This is the right-most route on the smaller grey wall. It features delicate climbing from the very beginning and has a crux dyno from two monos!
1 pitch (15 M), 5 bolts *FA: Aníbal Fernández & Josué Millo, 2003.*

② Tacto Rectal 7a+ ★★ .... ☐

Climb to the obvious flake, which you stand on to make the mono crux move.
1 pitch (15 M), 5 bolts *FA: Aníbal Fernández & Josué Millo, 2003.*

③ Príncipe Enano 7a+ ★★ .... ☐

A short, but explosive route!
1 pitch (15 M), 4 bolts *FA: Abel Pérez, 2003.*

④ Tiburón Siguato 6c ★ .... ☐

This line is close to the tree on the left. The anchor can be seen from the ground.
1 pitch (6 M), 4 bolts *FA: Aníbal Fernández, 2003.*

⑤ Bititi 6a+ ★★★ .... ☐

Bititi climbs the grey wall to the right of the dihedral. It starts by climbing to the top of the block attached to the wall just left of the tree.
1 pitch (17 M), bolts *FA: Aníbal Fernández, 2003.*

⑥ Pikín 6b+ ★★★★ .... ☐

Climb the inside corner. Don't be fooled, it's harder than it looks. This was the first route on the wall and was led ground-up with natural protection. At the crux, with only shaky pro below, the leader was stung on his forehead by a wasp. He managed not to fall and finished the first ascent onsight. His retribution was to return to bolt the climb, but it remains sporty with a highball start because someone stole the first hanger! The climbing is easy, but this section can be protected with small Tricams or wired nuts if desired.
1 pitch (20 M), 7 bolts *FA: Abel Pérez, 2002.*

⑦ Ana Banana 6c ★★★★ .... ☐

This excellent route climbs the centre of the overhanging left wall that forms the dihedral, and shares the same start as *Pikín*. The climbing is fun and sustained on jugs and has a sharp finish. It comes highly recommended!
1 pitch (22 M), 9 bolts *FA: Abel Pérez, 2002.*

⑧ Catamarán 7a+ ★★★★★ .... ☐

This route starts up the technical, grey arête left of *Ana Banana*. It finishes with a sustained and sharp section past the ledge.
1 pitch (20 M), bolts *FA: Josué Millo & Reiniel Sosa, 2005.*

⑨ El Salto de la Pelúa 6c+ ★★★ ..... ☐

This bouldery route vaults through the small overhang to the left of the dihedral. Clip the first bolt and get your belayer's attention before dynoing to the big jugs. A miss plus a nonchalant belay will most definitely equal a ground fall – this has happened with bone-breaking result. The grade depends on the height of the climber. At least one person has reached the jugs without *el salto* (the jump). Either way, it's a crowd-pleaser and fun to try!
1 pitch (10 M), 5 bolts *FA: Aníbal Fernández, 2003.*

⑩ Katja Me Punza 7a ★★ .... ☐

This route is left of *El Salto* on the same overhang. It has a painful mono move to surmount the initial section. Avoiding the mono may be possible, but raises the grade.
1 pitch (15 M), 7 bolts *FA: Aníbal Fernández, 2003.*

⑪ Dulce de Coco 6c ★★★ .... ☐

Start in the cavernous inside corner and tackle the first crux in a thin crack. This crack slowly widens over the little roof and is perfect for jamming, but the jagged nature of the rock may deter you.

I pitch (20 M), 9 bolts *FA: Aníbal Fernández, 2002.*

⑫ ¡Hay Mi Madre! 8a ★★ .... ☐

This climb is on the blank looking overhang left of the previous crack. It shares the belay with the next route.

I pitch (20 M), 7 bolts *FA: Yarobys García & José Luís Pimentel on Mother's Day, 2006.*

⑬ Rasta Crack 6b ★★★ .... ☐

Rasta Crack is just left of the cavernous inside corner. It starts with good holds to the first ledge and then finesses a cruxy section with smaller grips. Finish up a nice low angle crack past the small palm tree.

I pitch (20 M), bolts *FA: Aníbal Fernández, 2003.*

⑭ Aserejé 6a+ ★★★★ .... ☐

This route and the next two are located in the cavernous section just behind the big Jaguey tree. *Aserejé* starts on the easy ramp just off a block and climbs to a shelf. Pull over a small overhang and either continue up easier ground on the corrugated rib to the right or climb directly up the slightly harder face. It is very popular for the grade. *Aserejé* is "The Ketchup Song".

I pitch (20 M), bolts *FA: Aníbal Fernández & Alberto Leivas, 2003.*

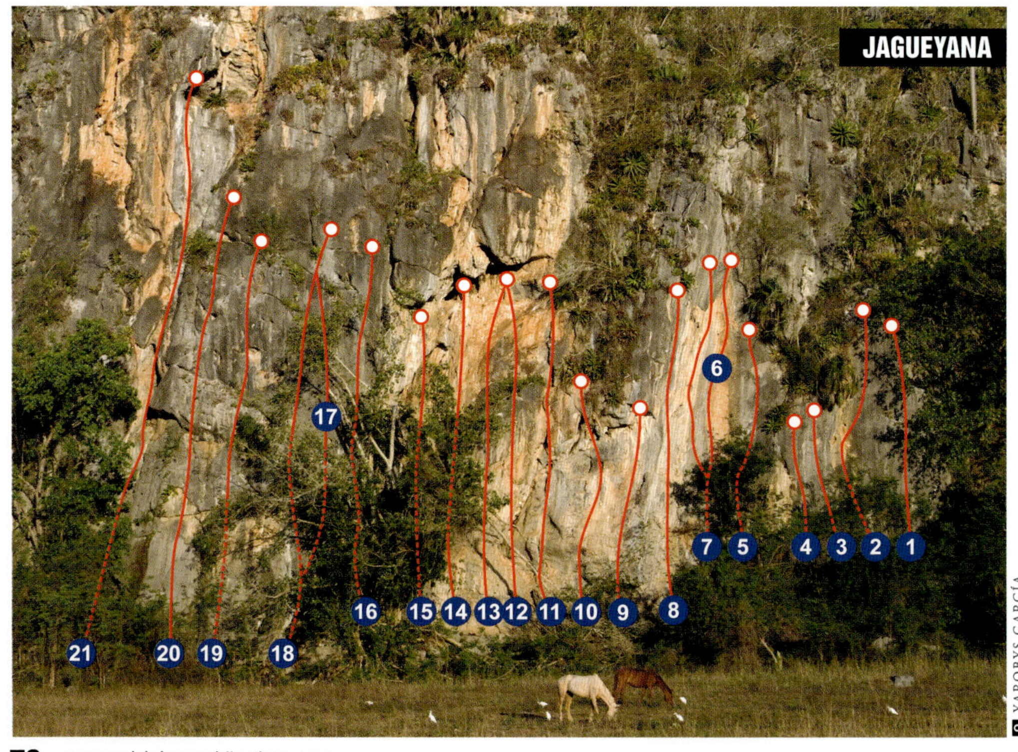

⑮ Lluvia de Meteoritos 6c ★★★ . . . . . ☐

Lluvia starts left of *Aserejé* and follows the chossy looking pillar of rock before moving onto a more solid face. The painful crux is just under the anchors. The name translates to "meteor showers".
1 pitch (20 M), bolts *FA: Josué Millo & Israel 2005.*

⑯ Brutus 7a+ ★★★★★ . . . . ☐

Brutus starts out a small roof with two bolts very close together. The crux comes above on the sustained, fat arête.
1 pitch (22 M), bolts *FA: Josué Millo & Adrián Pérez 2005.*

⑰ Arco de Josué 6b+ ★★★★ . . . . ☐

Start on the left edge of the cavernous groove, down at the farmland level. The line follows an arch that curves first to the right and then back to the left.
1 pitch (25 M), 10 bolts *FA: David Ryan & Josué Millo, 2005.*

⑱ Tubo de Roca 6b+ ★★★ . . . . ☐

This route uses the first two bolts of the previous one and climbs a half-pipe feature to the same anchors. The name translates to "rock tube".
1 pitch (20 M), 10 bolts *FA: Josué Millo & Adrián Pérez, 2004.*

⑲ Mister Feo 6c ★★★ . . . . ☐

This route is defined by the technical balance moves near the start. Be ready.
1 pitch (22 M), bolts *FA: Josué Millo & Fransua Bosmenier, 2004.*

⑳ Avalancha 6c+ ★★ . . . . ☐

Avalanche starts just left of the previous climb and is, unfortunately, a little dirty.
1 pitch (25 M), bolts *FA: Josué Millo & Fransua Bosmenier, 2004.*

Lunge! *Aníbal Fernández successfully completes the dyno on El Salto de la Pelua (6c+).*

㉑ Diana 6b ★★★ . . . . ☐

To find the start of this route you will have to walk a few metres back from the base of the wall and around the vegetation. It starts on low angle grey rock and climbs past the entrance of a fairly big cave, continuing up the inside corner. The crux is below the anchors, which are on a cave ledge. Be very cautious lowering as the route is *just* over 30 m.
1 pitch (33 M), bolts *FA: Aníbal Fernández & Reiniel Sosa, 2004.*

CUEVA LARGA

Cueva Larga – The Long Cave – is entirely hidden from view as it's a cleft-like hollow in the mountain formed by two closely-spaced parallel walls. Despite the narrow confines, the cliffs are significantly high with the left side reaching almost 100 m. This crag is a good choice for hot days since it's perpetually shaded, but this can occasionally attract mosquitoes so bring repellent. Also, since the cave is in such a dark recess, early morning and late afternoon sessions are a bad idea. The best light occurs from 11:00 AM–4:00 PM, so plan accordingly. Local trivia: One foreign visitor who eschewed the hospitality of Viñales' *casa particulares*, actually bivied in Cueva Larga. His routine involved climbing *La Cuevita* to a flat, airy ledge that generations of owls had padded with *egagrópilas* – little balls spat out by the owls with the bones and feathers of their prey!

APPROACH

From the base of La Yunta, walk about 15 metres to the left until you find a little trail that goes up into the trees. The trail turns right after a few metres into the entrance of Cueva Larga, which includes a three-metre downclimb. A 20-minute walk from Viñales.

THE CLIMBING

Cueva Larga has enough routes to keep you busy for days. The grades range from 3+ to 8a and include great warm-ups and brilliant moderates. Most of the routes are bolt protected single pitch, but there is one multi-pitch route for adventurous underground climbers and potential for more! The left wall features crimpy and technical lines and the right wall is blessed with impressive tufas like the majority of cliffs in Viñales. The popular routes are well buffed, but the rock quality on the flowstone can be a little dubious at times.

Amigos en el Tope, Ahora y Siempre (7c) *Small crimps lead out of the narrow chasm.*

Right Wall

This is the wall with the big tufas that's on the right side of the cave as you enter.

❶ Por Arriba del Bolt 7b ★★ . . . . ☐

This route and the next two are located at the entrance of the cave, right before you have to start the downclimb. *Por Arriba del Bolt* climbs the overhanging grey face. Watch the big crack underneath.
1 pitch (14 M), bolts *FA: Josué Millo, 2002.*

❷ Alcohólicos sin Fronteras 6a+ ★★ ☐

Start by stemming at the entrance of the cave then climb the small tufas on the right to a small ledge. Continue upwards by following the huecos.
1 pitch (15 M), bolts *FA: Aníbal Fernández, 2005.*

❸ Pelos de Rubia 6a ★★ . . . . ☐

Begin on the block. The name refers to a German climber that had feminine blonde hair.
1 pitch (15 M), bolts *FA: FA: Josué Millo, 2002.*

❹ Baja y Chupa 6b+ ★★★★ . . . . ☐

This route climbs the first tufa on the right, just after the finish of the downclimb. The first bolt is high.
1 pitch (25 M), bolts *FA: David Brasco, 2001.*

❺ Tetas Mediterraneas 6b+ ★★★★ . . ☐

Climb the obvious, rounded protrusions.
1 pitch (30 M), 15 bolts *FA: Vitalio Echazábal, 2001.*

❻ Chipojo 6a ★★★★★ . . . . ☐

This was the first route established in Cueva Larga. It climbs the first big column to a ledge and then follows the easy ramp to the left. For a harder, more direct finish, try the next route.
1 pitch (30 M), 14 bolts *FA: Aníbal Fernández & Fernando Paulete, 2001.*

❼ Papi 6b ★★★★ . . . . ☐

This variation of the upper section of *Chipojo/Chipojito* goes straight up from the ledge and then to the right on a crimpy face.
1 pitch, bolts *FA: Paul Laperrière & Markus Leicht, 2004.*

❽ Chipojito 6a ★★★★ . . . . ☐

Climb the second big column to the ledge and finish as *Chipojo*. Once you are standing on the ledge, back-clean the last quickdraw to avoid rope drag.
1 pitch (30 M), 13 bolts *FA: Vitalio Echazábal, 2001.*

❾ Contigo en la Distancia 7b ★★★★ ☐

Climb straight up past the small roof, heading for the long tufas higher on the wall. The bolts are far apart, but the falls are safe.
1 pitch (27 M), 8 bolts *FA: Paul Laperrière, Markus Leicht, & Josué Millo, 2002.*

❿ Fernando's Hideaway 6c ★★★★★ ☐

This fun multi-pitch route starts to the left of *Contigo en la Distancia*.
pitch 1 – 5 (10 M, 5 bolts) This pitch is often called *La Cuevita* and is a popular warm-up on its own. It climbs to the small cave and ledge. Once at the anchors, check out the view of the valley through the slot. This little tunnel is called "Cueva Lechuza" and has a parachute-shaped opening when seen from the other side.
pitch 2 – 6c (20 M, 6 bolts) Trend left.
pitch 3 – 5 (15 M, 4 bolts) Link this pitch with the previous pitch and watch for wasps behind you while climbing. To descend, have the belayer lower the leader down to the anchor on top of pitch 2. The leader then belays the second all the way to the top of pitch 3 and then lowers the second to the anchor on top of pitch 2. Pull the rope and rappel to the ground.
3 pitches, bolts *FA: Fernando Paulete, 2001.*

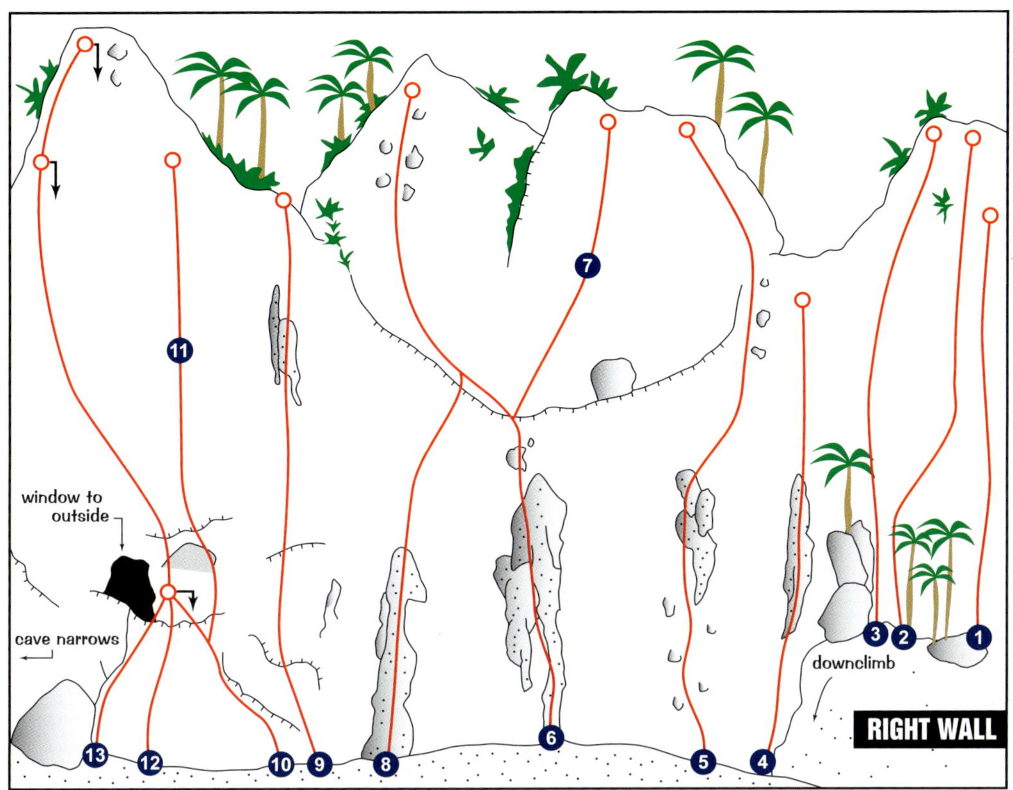

11 Jerry y Mirol 7a+ ★★★ . . . . ☐

This is a second pitch variation to *Fernando's Hideaway*. From the first anchor of that climb, step down and right and then go straight up the wall to an independent lowering station. Alternatively, start on *Hilo Dental* and climb directly up the wall in one long pitch.
1 pitch (27 M), 8 bolts *FA: Josué Millo & Alberto Leivas, 2002.*

12 Pelos en la Orilla 6b+ ★★★ . . . . ☐

This is a bouldery route that climbs the face under the anchors of *Fernando's Hideaway*.
1 pitch (14 M), 4 bolts *FA: Josué Millo & Alberto Leivas, 2003.*

13 Hilo Dental 6b+ ★★★ . . . . ☐

This is another short route that finishes at the *Fernando's Hideaway* anchor. Start by stemming between the boulder and the wall and then follow the crack to the anchors.
1 pitch (15 M), 5 bolts *FA: Aníbal Fernández & David Brasco, 2001.*

Left Wall

This is the wall that's on the left side of the cave as you enter. Routes are listed from left to right.

❶ La Vía Más Fácil de Cuba 3+ ★★ .. ☐

The name says it all – this is the easiest climb in Cuba. Start outside the entrance to Cueva Larga and climb up the left wall using slings on trees and rock features to protect yourself. A large tree up above serves as the anchor. Bring at least six slings.

1 pitch (15 M), Threads *FA: David Ryan & Armando Menocal, 2001.*

Maybe

❷ Disneylandia 4+ ★★★ . . . . ☐

Start right at the entrance to the cave and climb to the top of the boulder that is jammed between the two walls. Turn the corner and follow the tufa to the anchors.

1 pitch (15 M), bolts *FA: Josué Millo & Allison Andur, 2002.*

❸ Mambises y Maulets 6b+ ★★★★ .. ☐

This is the first route on the left wall after you enter Cueva Larga and make the downclimb. Climb the low angle wall, located two metres from the entrance, to a ledge with a tree. The crux is below the ledge. This and the next three routes are technical climbs that require more precise footwork than the other climbs in the area.

1 pitch (30 M), 12 bolts *FA: Eduard Viana & Carlos Pinelo, 2001.*

❹ Calzo de Guagua 7a ★★★★★ . . . . . ☐

This route is four metres right of *Mambises*. It features technical, sustained climbing and finishes at anchors right of the ledge. The bolts spacing is a little greater than usual.

1 pitch (30 M), bolts *FA: David Brasco & Aníbal Fernández, 2001.*

❺ Don Cojete de la Mancha 8a ★★★ . . . . ☐

This tough climb is two metres right of *Calzo*. It is technical has two very cruxys start. Both are about the same grade.

1 pitch (30 M), bolts *FA: Josué Millo & Adrián Pérez, 2002.*

❻ Amigos en el Tope, Ahora y Siempre 7c ★★★★★ . . . . ☐

This climb is very close to the previous route. It has an easier start that gives way to sustained crimps and small pinches.

1 pitch (30 M), 14 bolts *FA: Paul Laperrière & Markus Leicht, 2004.*

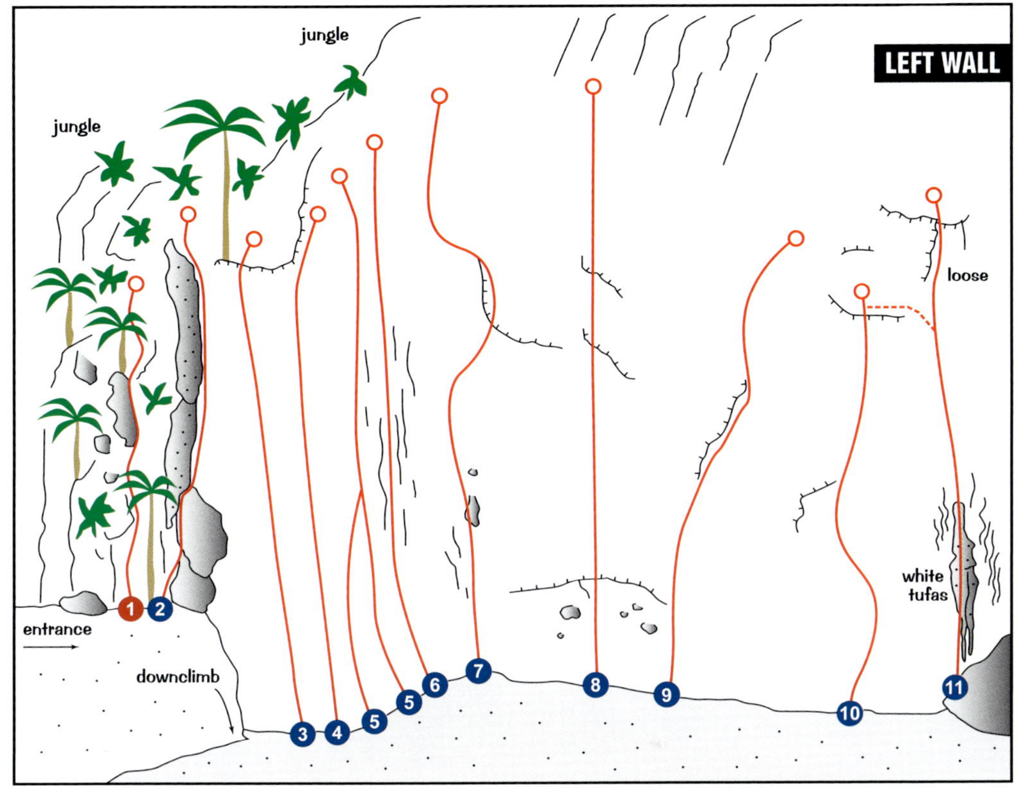

7 Maybe 7a ★★★★ . . . . ☐

Start to the right of *Amigos*. Climb to the big, restful hueco before the first crux. Next, traverse right to easier terrain and then back left before the final crux below the anchors.
1 pitch (30 M), bolts *FA: Josué Millo & Guro Ianssen, 2002.*

8 Contra la Espada y la Pared 7a+ ★★★★ . . . . ☐

Climb up the centre of the left wall. The bolts are hard to find at the base of the climb.
1 pitch (30 M), bolts *FA: Josué Millo & Alberto Leivas, 2002.*

9 Oculta Obsesión 6c ★★ . . . . ☐

This route climbs the dark red rock. The bolts are hard to find at the base of the route. Use the next two routes as a reference.
1 pitch (27 M), bolts *FA: Eduard Víana & Carlos Pinelo, 2001.*

10 On Belay Hombre 7a ★★★ . . . . ☐

This is the first route to the left of the white tufas at the end of Cueva Larga. The first bolts are hard to find – the hangers are brown.
1 pitch (20 M), 6 bolts *FA: David Ryan & Josué Millo, 2002.*

11 Leche de Mipalo 6c+ ★★★★ . . . . . . ☐

Climb the white tufa pinches. Lower from the anchors of the previous route to avoid the final section of loose rock.
1 pitch (30 M), bolts *FA: Aníbal Fernández & Loisbel Silveilo, 2005.*

LA YUNTA & GUAJIRO ECOLÓGICO

This is the closest cragging area to town and the routes described here occupy the south-facing wall of the Mogote del Valle, the mammoth sierra that dominates the landscape over Viñales. Rather than one continuous cliff, this area is comprised of sections of clean rock separated by vegetated patches. Since the majority of routes in this zone receive plenty of midday sun, it's better to climb here late in the afternoon or on cloudy days.

APPROACH

Follow one of the two roads that travel north out of Viñales. At first, the roads are paved, but quickly transition to dirt tracks and narrow footpaths. The red and grey striped walls of Guajiro Ecológico can be seen as you enter the farms and should help serve as a landmark. Please be respectful and minimize your impact when crossing the fields to the crags. The farmers plant crops very close to the cliffs and sometimes use the cavities in the rock to store tools. All these cliffs are about a 15-minute walk from Viñales.

THE CLIMBING

Most of the existing routes in this area are single pitch, but the obvious multi-pitch potential is now being explored by eager locals. The climbing here is typically very technical on vertical faces with small holds (one route has *six* monos), so if your back muscles are aching from stalactites-studded roofs, this zone might be the cure. All but two of the routes here are impeccably bolted (well-spaced, good placements, good anchors), but a few of the first hangers may be missing. This is usually because the local climbers can't keep up with the inscrutable thieves. (What do they do with a hanger and a nut anyway?)

Note: Wasps occupied these walls before climbers. The first route was named *Fire Down Below* because the climbers started a fire and climbed in a fog of smoke, wrongly thinking that it might deter the wasps. Since this technique failed, the main developers of the area, a Spanish-Cuban team, began bolting on lead armed with insecticide from the local campesinos, which seemed to work. Nowadays, all the well-travelled routes stay wasp-free, but on some of the less popular routes the wasps have returned. You've been warned.

Guajiro Ecologico Images *From top: Raúl Reyes plowing the fertile earth of his fields; Josué Millo strains on the crux of Carcharodón (7a+).*

La Yunta

This is the small wall at the left end of the sector that is separated by a fence from the rest of the routes. If you take the approach that starts on Salvador Cisneros street, this will be the first collection of routes you will find. Note that Cueva Larga is actually on the other side of this wall.

The Spanish word Yunta *means "ox team". The developers of this wall could hear the farmers below calling out the names of their oxen, Negrita and Jardinero, with a heavy accent on the last vowels. This provided inspiration for the names of three of the four routes, which are listed from left to right.*

❶ La Yunta 4+ ★ . . . . ☐

Climb the small blocky outcrop on the left edge of the wall.

1 pitch (14 M), 8 bolts FA: *Jorge Luís Mederos, 2001.*

❷ Jardinero 5 ★★★ . . . . ☐

This route follows an intermittent crack that angles to the right. Start just right of *La Yunta* and finish at the bolt anchors of *Jardinero*. Brings nuts and cams to two inches.

1 pitch (30 M), gear FA: *Fernando Paulete & Troy Stephens, 2001.*

❸ La Mulatísima 6a+ ★★★★ . . . . ☐

This and the next route have vegetated starts in a very small clearing about five metres to the right of *Jardinero*. *La Multatisima* is really just a bolted version of *Jardinero*. It was established because few of the locals owned the traditional gear necessary to climb *Jardinero* and it was on the verge of becoming extinct. *La Multatisima* is fully bolted and provides a direct start and finish to *Jardinero*, although it has a separate anchor.

1 pitch (30 M), 8 bolts FA: *Josué Millo & Armando Menocal, 2006.*

❹ Negrita 6a ★★★★ . . . . ☐

Start on the clean patch of rock to the right of the tree. Climb to the first ledge and then move to the right of the bolts. Head back left where it steepens.

1 pitch (30 M), 9 bolts FA: *Aníbal Fernández and Fernando Paulete, 2001.*

Guajiro Ecológico

This is the largest concentration of routes in this zone and the climbs are quite compressed in places. The wall stretches from the fence to the point at which the wall turns a corner before the Summertime alcove. The base of the first group of routes are behind a cafetal, *an orchard of coffee trees. Be careful not to bump or strike the trees when belaying and pulling ropes. Not only will you knock down the farmer's beans, but you may rain down "santanillás", little fire ants that are nearly invisible, but provide exceptionally painful and burning stings.*

© YAROBYS GARCÍA

⑤ Ostraman 6a ★★ . . . . ☐

The route follows the long, obvious crack which is inside the corner to the right of the fence. Due to the traditional protection required, this route receives little attention and wasps have recovered some terrain since the first ascent. If you do make it to the top, rap from the bolt anchor to threads on the tree (15 m) and from here to the ground (30 m). Permission to bolt this route has been granted by the first ascentionist. Bring nuts and wide-crack protection.

1 pitch (45 M), gear *FA: Aníbal Fernández & David Brasco, 2001.*

⑥ Habla Bien 7a+ ★★★ . . . . ☐

The first bolted line right of the crack.

1 pitch (30 M), bolts *FA: Josué Millo & Alberto Leivas, 2005.*

⑦ Peregrinos 6c ★★★ . . . . ☐

1 pitch (30 M), bolts *FA: Josué Millo & Alberto Leivas, 2005.*

⑧ Bejuco Colorado 7a+ ★★★★ . . . . . . ☐

The route starts next to the big palm. It has a delicate crux after the third bolt and a sustained right-facing corner that arches to the anchors on the ledge. The second pitch has not yet been done.

1 pitch (30 M), bolts *FA: David Brasco & Rosa Catalá, 2001.*

⑨ Vida Ingrata 7c ★★★ . . . . ☐

The route starts up the face and joins the last bolts of *Bejuco Colorado*.

1 pitch (30 M), bolts *FA: Josué Millo & Alberto Leivas, 2005.*

⑩ Vibración Interior 8a ★★ . . . . ☐

This is a harder variation that climbs the face and also joins the last bolts of *Bejuco Colorado*.
1 pitch (30 M), bolts *FA: Josué Millo & Alberto Leivas, 2005.*

⑪ Polvo Piojillo 6b+ ★★★★ . . . . ☐

Start with the little roof at the base of the left-facing corner and then move left onto the face to *Bejuco Colorado's* anchor.

1 pitch (30 M), bolts *FA: David Brasco & Rosa Catalá, 2001.*

⑫ Carcharodón 7a+ ★★★★ . . . . ☐

Start one metre right of the previous route. After moving over the initial roof, prepare for hard face climbing on sharp rock. *Carcharodon* means teeth of the tiger shark.

1 pitch (25 M), bolts *FA: David Brasco & Rosa Catalá, 2001.*

⑬ Ranas Pelúas (p1) 6c+ ★★★★ . . . . ☐

This is a nice climb that starts on the tufa above the little roof. Shares an anchor with *Carcharodon*.

1 pitch (25 M), 7 bolts *FA: David Brasco, Rosa Catalá & Nivaldo Díaz, 2001.*

⑭ La Pareja Explosiva 8a? . . . . ☐

This route is a second pitch project that climbs left from the *Carcharodon/Ranas* anchor.

1 pitch (28 M), 11 bolts *FA: Alberto Leivas & Yarobys García, 2007.*

⑮ Ranas Pelúas (p2) 6c ★★ . . . . ☐

This route is also a second pitch off the *Carcharodon/Ranas* anchor, but it goes right.

1 pitch (22 M), 9 bolts *FA: Alberto Leivas & Yarobys García, 2007.*

⑯ El Fantasma de la Ópera 6a ★★★★★ . . . . ☐

This is the popular warm-up for the crag and starts under the right side of the small roof. The second pitches (6b to the left and 6b+ to the right) are great additions to the initial pitch. They finish on top of the big stalactite!

1 pitch (25 M), 9 bolts *FA: Alberto Leivas & Yarobys García, 2007.*

17 La Vida es Bella 7a ★★★★★ . . . . . . ☐

This route shares an anchor with the previous one and climbs the harder face to the right. There is a thin, technical crux midway up.
1 pitch (25 M), 8 bolts *FA: Josué Millo & Jordi Tejero, 2002.*

18 Muerte Blanca 6b ★★★★ . . . . ☐

This route climbs the big tufa. In the tradition of the crag, many wasps died attempting to defend this piece of stone.
1 pitch (20 M), 9 bolts *FA: Yarobys García & Fransuá Bosmenier, 2007.*

19 Psicosis 6c ★★★★★ . . . . ☐

The highest climb on the crag features three great moderate pitches (6b, 6c, 6a+). The first pitch follows the wide crack and a single, 60-metre rope is enough for the rappels.
3 pitches, bolts *FA: Josué Millo & J. Blanco, 2002.*

20 Salta Pa' lo Chapeáo 7a+ ★★★ . . . . ☐

A more difficult option follows the face left of the crack to reach the same anchor as *Psicosis*.
1 pitch (20 M), bolts *FA: Josué Millo & Adrián Pérez.*

21 Cusacutuza 6a ★★★ . . . . ☐

This pitch follows a few cracks. It was likely the first gear-protected climb done in the area and was originally named *Fire Down Below*.
1 pitch (19 M), bolts *FA: Frank Zacheri & Paul Tichner, 2000.*

22 El Beso de la Avispa 7b+ ★★★★ . . . ☐

Hard moves on the grey rock.
1 pitch (20 M), 9 bolts *FA: Martín Moline & Ariel Pascualetti.*

23 El Hombre y la Tierra 6c+ ★★★ . . . ☐

This route starts in the small alcove and climbs overhanging cracks to an independent anchor.
1 pitch (25 M), 8 bolts *FA: Josué Millo & Julién.*

24 Julia Merece 6a ★★★ . . . . ☐

Climbs the next cracks to the right of the previous route and shares the belay.
1 pitch (25 M), bolts *FA: Josué Millo & Julien.*

25 Josué's Route 6a ★★★ . . . . ☐

Another moderate crack.
1 pitch (25 M), bolts *FA: Josué Millo, 2002.*

26 Avispicidio 6b+ ★★★★ . . . . ☐

Climbs a thin crack on the overhang.
1 pitch (15 M), 5 bolts *FA: David Brasco & Aníbal Fernández, 2001.*

27 Los Putre 6a ★★ . . . . ☐

This short route starts on the face just right of the *Avispicidio* crack.
1 pitch (15 M), 5 bolts *FA: Yarobys García, Roilandy, & Daniel, 2006.*

Malaje Wall

The next routes are found past the next vegetated patch, moving right, where the wall clears again. Some bullet holes are found at the base of this wall and curiously mix with the many natural monos.

28 Los Picapiedras 6c ★★★★ . . . . ☐

This route links monos and small edges. The name translates to "The Flintstones".
1 pitch (15 M), bolts *FA: Adrián Pérez.*

29 Malaje 6c+ ★★★★ . . . . ☐

This route also features small edges, but follows the half-pipe dihedral.
1 pitch (25 M), bolts *FA: David Brasco & Nivaldo Díaz, 2001.*

30 Una Larga Amistad con Dos Bolas de Cariño 6b ★★★ . . . . ☐

This line tackles the obvious left-facing crack.
1 pitch (25 M), bolts *FA: David Brasco & Nivaldo Díaz, 2001.*

19
14 15 16 16 19
5
6 7 8 9 10 11 12 13 16 17 18 19 20 21 22 23 24 25 26 27
GUAJIRO ECOLÓGICO

🟢31 **La Goropeza 6c** ★★★ . . . . ☐

Climb the face to the right of the crack.
1 pitch (25 M), 9 bolts *FA: Yarobys García & Yandy, 2007.*

Por Tu Culpa Wall

The next three routes are a few more metres to the right on a small clean wall.

🔵32 **Burdel de Sangre 6c** ★★ . . . . ☐

Start on the face under a small cave.
1 pitch (15 M), 3 bolts *FA: Pimentel brothers.*

🔵33 **¡Por Tu Culpa! 7a** ★★★ . . . . ☐

1 pitch (20 M), bolts *FA: Pimentel brothers.*

🔵34 **Unknown** . . . . ☐

1 pitch, bolts *FA: Unknown.*

Zapatá Wall

The next three routes are on the little wall behind the coconut tree. They all share the top section.

🔵35 **Dos Empotres 6a** ★★★ . . . . ☐

1 pitch (15 M), 5 bolts *FA: Alberto Leivas, 2007.*

🔵36 **No Te Vistas que No Vas 6b+** ★★★ ☐

1 pitch (15 M), 5 bolts *FA: Alberto Leivas & Pedro Luís, 2007.*

🔵37 **Zapatá 7a** ★★★★ . . . . ☐

This is the last route to the right, behind the coconut tree and below Summertime alcove.
1 pitch (17 M), 6 bolts *FA: Alberto Leivas & Pedro Luís, 2007.*

Summertime Alcove

All the previous routes start from the level of the farmland. This alcove is just above the alley level to the right of the orange wall. The routes here are steeper than on Guajiro Ecológico.

🔵38 **Cuando el Mal es de Cagar 7b+** ★★★★★ . . . . ☐

From behind the coconut tree, scramble uphill

MALAJE WALL

POR TU CULPA WALL

to the right until you reach the ledge – belay here. The route starts up a dihedral.

1 pitch (25 M), 8 bolts *FA: Alberto Leivas & Yarobys García, 2007.*

39 Mis Dos Spits 6c+ ★★★★★ . . . . ☐

This is a great climb! It starts at the base of the corner and features steep huecos. Two pitches: 6c+ (30 M) and 6b (20 M).

2 pitches, bolts *FA p1: Josué Millo & Helmut Gargitter, 2002.*

40 Medio Bandido 7b+ ★★★★★ . . . . . . ☐

Prepare for a hard crux on the overhanging face at the start, just right of the corner.

1 pitch (30 M), bolts *FA: Helmut Gargitter & Paul Trenkwalder, 2001.*

41 Intrusos 6a ★★★★★ . . . . ☐

Climb the obvious, continuous tufas that start in the back of the alcove.

1 pitch (15 M), 6 bolts *FA: Yarobys García & Alberto Leivas, 2007.*

42 Polaca de Oro 6c+ ★★ . . . . ☐

This route starts on the right side of the alcove. It follows a reddish face before moving into a crack and up the right-hand wall. The crux is a bit dirty.

1 pitch (20 M), bolts *FA: Aníbal Fernández & Josué Millo, 2004.*

43 Summertime 7a ★★★★★ . . . . ☐

This is a fine climb that starts well below the previous routes, at the base of the right-hand wall, left of the big tree. It follows the obvious crack and is easy until the roof at the very top, which is the crux. Perhaps an anchor at that point will be added to create another moderate climb.

1 pitch (30 M), bolts *FA: Aníbal Fernández & Yarobys García, 2004.*

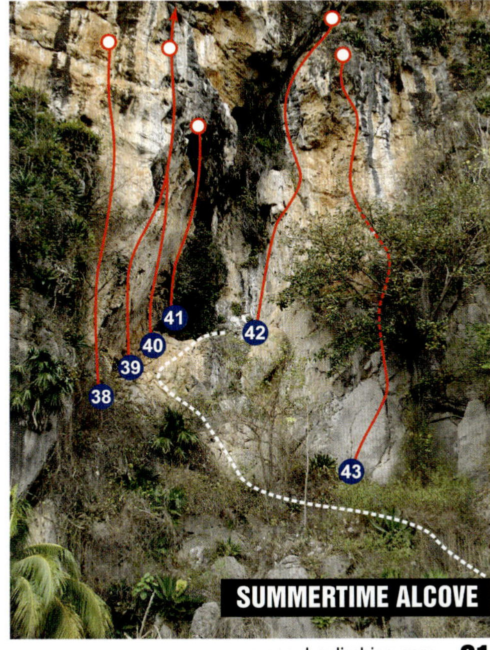

PARED DE LOS TORMENTOS

Pared de los Tormentos is a large wall that lies between Guajiro Ecológico and Milenio, right at the corner of the Mogote del Valle. You shouldn't have a problem finding it as you can clearly see the two, very distinct bands of grey rock that both contain three-pitch routes. The Tormentos are in sun during most of the day, so wait for clouds or climb late in the afternoon.

APPROACH

The best approach is through Raúl's farm – the wall is clearly visible to the west. Walk across the fields and take the trail that enters the forest a few metres left of the obvious, big boulder. Upon reaching the base of the talus, wander under the vegetation for a few metres until you come to the wall. The initial bolts are obvious and the two routes are easy to differentiate. This cliff is about a 20-minute walk from Viñales.

THE CLIMBING

This wall features two enjoyable, multi-pitch routes at very accessible grades. The climbs both have good exposure on friendly, not-too-steep terrain (by Viñales standards, anyway) and are very well-bolted. The rock is on the sharp side, so tread delicately and be cautious of handling the vegetation as *Guao* (Cuban poison ivy) is around the approach and the walls. The name *Tormentos* (Spanish for "torments") refers to the heavy gardening and multiple hazards encountered on the first ascent of the wall.

Más Tarde (6b) *Two different views of the excellent rock and position on this popular multi-pitch climb.*

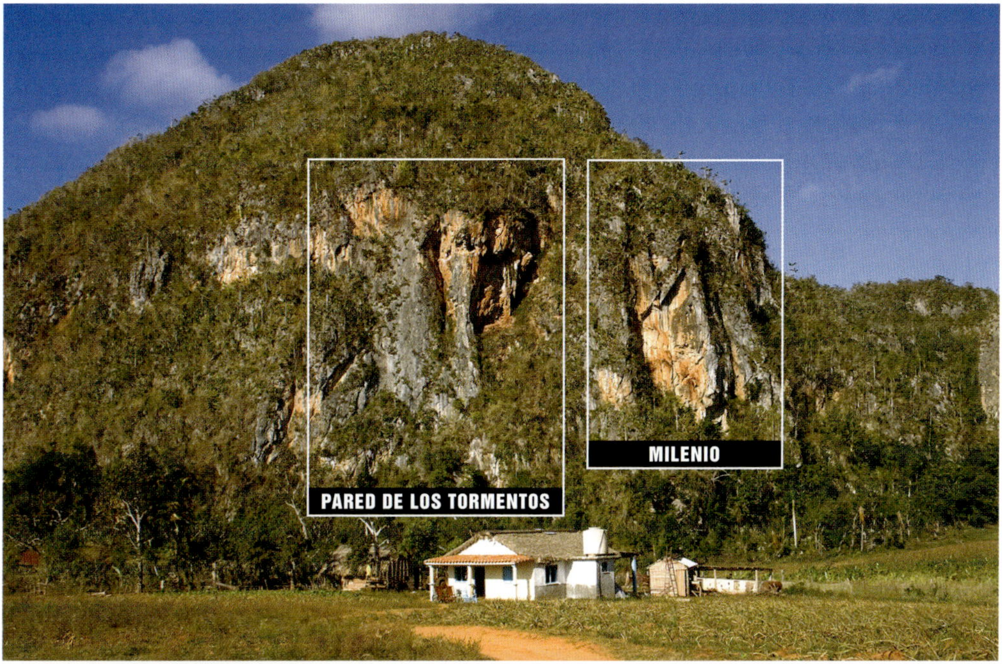

YAROBYS GARCÍA

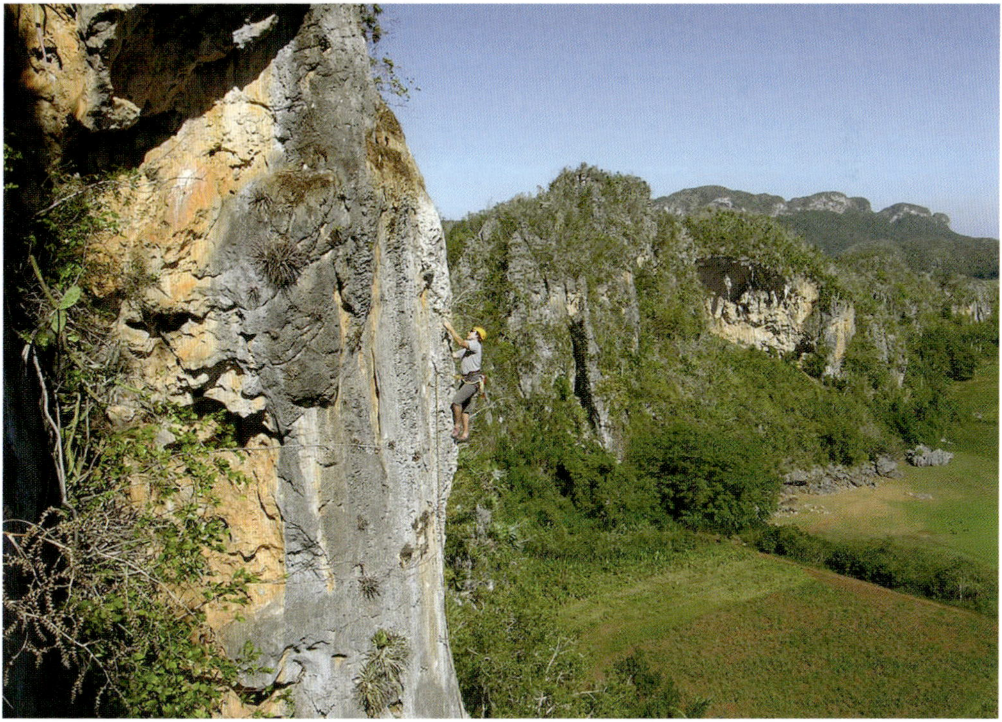

PAUL LAPERIÈRRE

Pared de los Tormentos

Routes are listed from left to right.

❶ Guao, Guano y Espinas 6a ★★★ ..☐

This is the three-pitch route up the long, grey wall. The first two pitches are low angle climbing, but the third gets quite steep. As you climb, it will become obvious that the first ascent involved some hard-core vertical gardening! You can rappel the first two pitches with a single 60-metre rope, but to get down from the third, bring a 70-metre rope or an extra cord. All the stations are well-bolted, but you might want to replace old slings since the wall gets a lot of nylon-cooking sun.

pitch 1 (6a, 20 M, 5 bolts)
pitch 2 (6b, 30 M, 10 bolts)
pitch 3 (6b, 30 M, 12 bolts)
3 pitches, bolts *FA: Fernando Paulette, Carlos Pinelo & David Ryan, 2001.*

❷ Más Tarde 6b+ ★★★ . . . .☐

This is the multi-pitch route on the right side of the formation that finishes up the orange streaked wall. The grade on all three pitches is consistent, but the third pitch is the steepest and most spectacular. This route has a nice ambience and a stunning last belay in a brilliant setting!

pitch 1 (6b+, 25 M)
pitch 2 (6b, 30 M)
pitch 3 (6b, 27 M)
3 pitches, bolts *FA: Paul & André Laperrière, 2005.*

Más Tarde (6b) *Enjoying spectacular views of the lush fields below from the final belay.*

© JIMMY CHIN

1
2
PARED DE LOS TORMENTOS

MILENIO

This is the beautiful red and gold wall visible on the left upon entering Raúl's farm. Two diagonal dihedrals are noticeable near the top and make the cliff very easy to locate. Considering this wall stays in the shade most of the day, it's interesting it receives very little traffic. There are two plausible explanation for this: the traditional protection required on many of the pitches and the small base area, which doesn't accommodate groups. Regardless, the lack of visitors is a shame because these routes are of very high quality.

APPROACH

The trail to Milenio follows a steep line under the wall amongst the coffee trees (please don't pull on the plants). You will reach the crag at the alcove of *Milenio* and *Huevos Verdes con Jamón*. This cliff is about a 20-minute walk from Viñales.

THE CLIMBING

Although the nature of the routes vary on this wall, they tend to follow interesting, natural features that give them a more "traditional" feel then the common straight-up-the-face sport lines found elsewhere. The quality of the rock is generally very good, but since the lines weave around and often follow cracks, do use some caution. Many of the pitches on the wall require gear, but there is a bolted testpiece for those feeling sporty!

Huevos Verdes con Jamon (6c+) *Aníbal Fernández enjoys spectacular scooped rock on pitch 2.*

Milenio

Routes are listed from left to right.

❶ Living la Vía Loca 6b ★★★ . . . . ☐

This is a nice, well-protected crack climb, but it sees little traffic because the approach options are poor – bushwhacking along the base or traversing left from *Milenio's* first belay are the only ways to reach the start. Bring nuts and camming devices to three inches.
1 pitch (30 M), gear *FA: Aníbal Fernández & Jorge Mederos, 2000.*

❷ Milenio 7a+ ★★★ . . . . ☐

Milenio is the original route on this wall and makes for a great outing. This route has bolts, but requires supplemental gear. Bring small Tricams, hexes and cams to three inches.
pitch 1 (6b, 20 M, 1 Bolt) The first pitch starts on the white face on the left of the alcove. Look for a bolt about five metres from the

© BETH WALD

ground. After you clip it, follow the overhanging cracks, placing your own protection. Belay from bolts.
pitch 2 (6b+, 25 M) Follow more gear-protected cracks up and left of the anchor. Get into a chimney and then exit onto a ledge. Execute the crux and then traverse left following a diagonal ledge (loose rock) to a hanging belay.
pitch 3 (7a+, 15 M) The last pitch is bolted and climbs a beautiful overhanging dihedral with a crux as you leave the belay. Descend by rappelling 30 metres to *A Mulatazo Limpio's* first station and then 30 metres to the ground.
3 pitches, mixed *FA: Vitalio Echazábal & Aníbal Fernández, 2000.*

❸ A Mulatazo Limpio 7a ★★★★ . . . . . ☐

This pitch climbs the bolted wide cracks at the base of the wall to the right. It goes past a small dark roof and then straight up through the overhang to an athletic finish.
1 pitch (30 M), bolts *FA: Aníbal Fernández & David Brasco, 2000.*

**❹ Huevos Verdes
con Jamón 6c+ ★★★★ . . . . ☐**

This a good route, but the top of the first pitch and the first half of the second have some loose rock. If you avoid the flakes and use the many huecos, it's not a problem.
pitch 1 (6b, 30 M, 11 bolts) Start up *A Mulatazo Limpio*, but avoid the final overhang by taking an easier line to the right.
pitch 2 (6c+, 30 M, 13 bolts) Climb up past the caves and onto a ramp. Follow this to the top and a junction with *Milenio* at the anchor. Descend as for *Milenio*.
2 pitches, bolts *FA: Aníbal Fernández & Vitalio Echazábal, 2000.*

❺ ¡Hay Papito! 8a ★★★★★ . . . . ☐

This route draws strong climbers – it requires power and technique. Unconfirmed grade.
1 pitch (30 M), 10 bolts *FA: David Brasco, 2001.*

MILENIO

ENSENADA DE RAÚL

La Ensenada de Raúl is a small, hidden valley in the mogotes behind Raúl Reyes' farm. This area contains the highest number of moderate grade routes in Viñales and is a an excellent starting point for visiting or neophyte climbers. Crops are grown in this area, so care must be taken when hiking between the cliffs. The term *ensenada* loosely translates to mean "cove" or "bay".

The routes in the *ensenada* are clustered in small groups on crags scattered around the edge of the little valley. Some of these crags are easily recognizable, such as Punta Repaso and Punta Lider, but others are hidden behind the trees. The different orientations of the cliffs allow you to pick shaded routes at any time of the day.

APPROACH

From Raúl Reyes' farm you can easily spot the entrance to the *ensenada* just left of the Arista Filo de Cuchilla. To approach, walk past Raúl's house to the north end of the farm and pass through the gate. Turn left and follow a trail toward Filo de Cuchilla; the rocky uphill path will bring you directly into the *ensenada*. Once inside, the prominent white wall to the left is Punta Repaso and the lonely little mogote in front of you is Punta Lider. All these cliffs are about a 30-minute walk from Viñales.

THE CLIMBING

Expect lots of nice moderates on sharpish rock with a bit of jungle touring necessary to get around. The climbs are well-bolted and there are lots of enjoyable options, even for first-timers. There are a couple of 30-metre pitches, but most of the lines are relatively short.

Torre Menoco *Reaching the summit on the interesting spire that lies above the approach trail to Ensenada de Raúl.*

MILENIO
ENSENADA DE RAUL
ARISTA FILO DE CHUCHILLA

N
100m = 5cm
Cueva Cabeza de la Vaca
Torre Menoco
Filo de Chuchilla
ENSENADA DE RAUL
Dos Palmas
TORRE BLANCA
PUNTA LIDER
MURALLA PITÚ
Milenio
RAUL'S FARM
PUNTA REPASO
MOGOTE   DEL   VALLE
Los Tormentos

Muralla Pitú

Once inside the ensenada, the crags are described in a clockwise fashion. Muralla Pitú is the first cliff on the left and is approximately 60 metres left of Punta Repaso. Muralla Pitú is hard to see from the main trail because the vegetation conceals it, but as you approach, the clearing at its base becomes readily apparent. Pitú is the shallow dihedral in the centre. This cliff is slabby and gets all-day shade. No photograph.

❶ Comiquita 6a ★★★ . . . . □

The first bolted line is about 2 metres left of *Pitú*.

1 pitch (20 M), bolts *FA: Josué Millo, 2005.*

❷ Pitú 6a ★★★ . . . . □

This is the line that reaches the top dihedral.

1 pitch (20 M), 6 bolts *FA: Aníbal Fernández, 2001.*

❸ Mojaita 5+ ★★★ . . . . □

This is the line a few metres to the right.

1 pitch (20 M), bolts *FA: Reinier Sosa, 2005.*

Punta Repaso

This is the 30 metre-tall white wall that you first see on the left when you enter the ensenada. The longest routes of the area are found here. This cliff gets morning sun and the climbing is vertical.

❶ El Puso el Bolt 4+ ★★ . . . . □

This route has an intermediate anchor for people to practice multi-pitch techniques. It climbs the most vegetated line to the left.

1 pitch (30 M), bolts *FA: Vitalio Echazábal & Carlos Pinelo, 2001.*

❷ Ojos Carmelitas 5+ ★★★★ . . . . □

A nice climb for the grade.

1 pitch (30 M), bolts *FA: Neil Gresham, 2002.*

❸ El Repaso 5 ★★★★ . . . . □

Steep and sustained for the grade.

1 pitch (25 M), 9 bolts *FA: Vitalio Echazábal, 2001.*

Punta Lider

This is the lonesome, small mogote in the middle of the ensenada, with a short wall. It is sunny all day and the climbing is slabby.

❶ Guides Route 4+ ★★ . . . . □

This is the route on the left that climbs close to the edge of the arête. The Cubans call the route "Lider".

1 pitch (12 M), 3 bolts *FA: David Ryan, Armando Menocal & Scott Cole, 2000.*

❷ Ratoncita Pérez 4 ★★ . . . . □

This route and the next one share the same top anchor. Both are very easy climbs.

1 pitch (14 M), 4 bolts *FA: Josué Millo, 2005.*

❸ Cucarachón 4 ★★ . . . . □

The route on the right.

1 pitch (14 M), 4 bolts *FA: Reinel Sosa & Junior González, 2005.*

❹ Dos Palmás 5+ ★★★ . . . . □

This nice face climb is a lonely route hidden in the back of the *ensenada*. Follow the trail to the right of Punta Lider, circling to the left until you find a shady white wall with bolts and two distinct palms on the upper part.

1 pitch, bolts *FA: David Ryan & Paul Tichner, 2000.*

Torre Blanca

This is another wall hidden behind the trees. As you enter the ensenada, it is on the right. The routes may be confusing. Try to find the climb Torre Blanca first a as reference. This cliff features all-day shade and vertical climbing. No photograph.

❶ Torre Blanca 5+ ★★★ ....☐

This route climbs a light grey pillar with a vertical column that towers slightly above and apart from the rest of the wall.

1 pitch (15 M), 4 bolts *FA: David Ryan & Paul Tichner, 2000.*

❷ Torreando 5+ ★★ ....☐

This is the route just left of the pillar that climbs the dihedral before moving onto the upper face.

1 pitch (14 M), bolts *FA: Josué Millo & Yarobys García, 2004.*

❸ Eternos Jóvenes 4+ ★★★ ....☐

This is the left-most route on the wall, about 30 metres left of the *Torre* pillar. The start is almost at the corner.

1 pitch (21 M), 3 bolts *FA: Scott Cole, 2001.*

❹ Psicología Infantil 5+ ★★★ ......☐

Climb the dihedral right of the pillar

1 pitch (12 M), bolts *FA: Josué Millo & Adrián Pérez, 2004.*

❺ En la Sombrita 4+ ★★★ ....☐

This route shares an anchor with the previous one and starts just left of the ficus tree.

1 pitch (12 M), bolts *FA: Josué Millo & Adrián Pérez, 2004.*

❻ Otra Pasta 5 ★★★ ....☐

Starts to the right of the ficus tree.

1 pitch (17 M), bolts *FA: Yarobys García & Josué Millo, 2004.*

❼ Invernando 6a+ ★★★ ....☐

This is the line that climbs the offwidth crack, an uncommon rock feature for Viñales.

1 pitch (15 M), bolts *FA: Yarobys García & Josué Millo, 2004.*

PUNTA REPASO

PUNTA LIDER

ARISTA FILO DE CUCHILLA

Arista Filo de Cuchilla – The Razor's Edge Buttress – is visible from the entrance to Raúl's farm. The evident grey arête and pointy tip make it easy to spot from a distance. Despite being sunny, sharp, windy and vegetated, this crag remains home to the most popular two-pitch route on the Mogote del Valle!

APPROACH

After passing through Raúl's farm, turn left and head up the trail toward the Ensenada de Raúl. When level with the base of the buttress, follow a short horizontal trail to the right. This cliff is about a 20-minute walk from Viñales.

THE CLIMBING

It's certainly worth a look as there are seven pitches of "twisted beauty" on this wall. The routes follow natural lines with good exposure for their grades, but the rock is the sharpest you will ever climb on. Despite this, the combination of ultra-honed stone and moderate climbing can make the routes feel like a lot of fun! The buttress is 50 metres at its highest point and is actually one of the few crags with a walk-down descent along the back-side, although most people still prefer to rappel. This wall gets lots of midday sun, but shade can be found early in the morning and again late in the afternoon.

Filo de Chuchilla (6a+) *Daniel Duane on the sharp but excellent stone of the "Razor's Edge".*

❶ Freebies 4+ ★★ ....☐

This route is on the lower wall left of the main arête and starts practically in the *ensenada*. There are no bolts; you'll have to protect it with nuts, Tricams and threads. To descend, lower from an in-situ piece of webbing with a carabiner, which may need replacing.
1 pitch (30 M), gear *FA: Fernando Paulete, 2001.*

❷ Mi Chica Metálica 6a ★★★ ....☐

This is the first, fully bolted route to the left of the arête.
pitch 1 (6a, 25 M) A long pitch tackles the grey wall.
pitch 2 (6a, 15 M) A shorter pitch leads to the top.
2 pitches, bolts *FA: Adrián Pérez & Fransua Bosmenir, 2006.*

❸ Marcelino Pan, y se Vino 6a ★★★ ☐

This is an optional first pitch for *Filo de Cuchilla* and starts right below the second pitch arête. There is a small overhang with a sharp crack in the first few metres of the pitch and then it wanders through the bromeliads.
1 pitch (30 M), bolts *FA: Josué Millo, 2002.*

❹ Filo de Cuchilla 6a+ ★★★★★ ......☐

Filo de Cuchilla is the original "Razor's Edge". Some disagree with the rating because of the cutting rock, but it is a classic of the less-than-overhanging-grey-limestone variety and definitely a must-do route for climbers curious about karst climbing. Bring 12 quickdraws.
pitch 1 (6a+, 25 M, 11 bolts): Begin on the right end of the base, just before the vegetation. Climb the clean face and traverse left before you reach the plants. The anchors are to the right of the small tree on the ledge.
pitch 2 (6a, 30 M, 10 bolts): This is the route's signature pitch and climbs the exposed arête to the top, but the last few metres are runout. To descend, walk down the back of the buttress following an improbable trail. Alternatively, rappel the route, 50 metres to the ground or 25 metres to the first belay station. If you tie two ropes together, ensure the knot will not get caught on the rock edge when you pull the ropes.
2 pitches, bolts *FA: David Ryan, Armando Menocal & Carlos Pinelo, 2000.*

❺ Hara Kiri 6b ★★★ ....☐

This is a harder (and sharper) variation to the second pitch of *Filo*. It shares the first bolt of the second pitch and then follows the independent line of bolts up the face to finish at the same top anchors.
1 pitch (25 M), bolts *FA: Aníbal Fernández, 2001.*

Filo de Cuchilla *Josué Millo in action.*

Ensenada
de Raul
1
2
3
4
5
4

TORRE MENOCO

This partially-hidden karst tower is found at the back of Raúl's farm, between Ariesta Filo de Cuchilla and Cabeza de la Vaca. From the trail, the tower looks covered with bromeliads (a large family of flowering plants native to the tropical Americas), but the cleanest face is hidden from view. Regardless, the climbing still has a bit of a jungle-like feel. Interestingly, the cliff was first discovered by Josué Millo and Armando Menocal. They named it Torre Menoco, but later gave it a tongue-in-cheek nickname, "Torre La Muerte de Menoco" (The Tower of Menocal's Death). This was because the eponymous Menocal had, by then, essentially become "dead" to Cuba. In other words, he was banned entry into the country.

APPROACH:

Head across Raúl's farm and through the gate as if heading for the Ensenada de Raúl. Instead of turning left or right, head directly toward the Torre Menoco wall, around a large Jaguey (the tree with the aerial roots) and then ascend to the left of the base of the tower. The approach takes about 20 minutes from Viñales.

THE CLIMBING

The routes are generally moderate on rock that ranges from sharp to very sharp! The big draw to this cliff is the fantastic view and a vertical "botanical tour" with great exposure. Keep your rope and your knees away from the predatory edges and mind the plants; they were there long before us.

Torre Menoco Front

The first climb is on the front of the tower.

❶ El Asegurador Cuenta 4+ ★★★ . . . ☐

This is the normal route up Torre Menoco and you'll find the first bolts at the start of the ridge on the left side of the tower. The route climbs the ridge, following the cleanest line between the plants. Bring some long slings to keep your rope away from the bloodthirsty corners. Although it's two pitches, they can be linked with 16 quickdraws and a 60-metre rope. The belay at the summit is a bed of nails on the most unforgiving *diente de perro* (dog's fangs) you will ever touch. To descend, rappel the back side of the tower (30 metres) and scramble down the trail that goes around the tower clockwise. Some brief bushwhacking is involved.

1 long pitch (55 M), 9 bolts *FA: Josué Millo & Armando Menocal, 2005.*

Torre Menoco Back

*These two routes are located on the back of the tower. As you rappel from the previous route you can see the bolts on the face. Most people climb El Asegurador first, since the rappel drops you right at the start of these lines. Otherwise you will have to circle around the **right** side of the tower until you reach the base of the clean wall.*

❷ Atalaya 6b ★★★★ . . . . ☐

As you face the wall, this is the line on the right.

1 pitch (20 M), 8 bolts *FA: Josué Millo, 2005.*

❸ Siete Bolts para Mi Niño 6b ★★ . . . ☐

This route starts two metres left of *Atalaya*

1 pitch (20 M), 7 bolts *FA: Josué Millo 2005.*

"Seriously now, how much do you want this one, Neil?" asked the British photographer and climber Mike "Mikey" Robertson.

"…Err, quite a lot, I think!"

"Right, well we're going to have to go for it then, aren't we?"

"Are you sure you're alright to…?"

Before I could talk him out of it, Mikey was off. A huge wave of limestone reared over our heads at a continuous angle of 45 degrees, its underside laced with tufas and stalactites. Our target was to bolt our way up to the giant dangling stalactite at 60 feet and from there onwards to the top. We learnt quickly that bolting on abseil is rarely an option in Cuba – not even Indiana Jones would make it through the poison ivy-infested jungle that surrounds almost every worthwhile piece of rock. So, with our cordless Hilti connected to a zip line, and in full aiding apparel, Mikey set to it. At this stage it was much easier to ignore the fact that the limestone to the right of our line was a nice familiar orangey grey colour and the limestone to the left was a rather alien looking browny black. The reason for this was because our chosen line delineated the boundary of the world's largest wasps' nest! Within arms reach of Mikey, every spare inch of rock was encrusted with evil hanging nests, some of them abandoned, but most of them alive and swarming. Mikey freed a move or two, placed a wobbly wire in a pocket and then threw a sling around a tufa.

"OK, take me there and send her up," called Mikey.

We'd tested the drill for volume and resonance at ground level and we hadn't disturbed the wasps, but Mikey was closer to them now.

"Get ready to lower," he muttered.

Deep breath, and the first anchor went in. I noticed that the higher he proceeded from here, the closer our route was getting to the "black line". At 50 feet they started circling him. Mikey placed a skyhook in a tiny pocket and surveyed the scene.

"I need to drill about 4 inches from a nest – it's not going to happen."

"OK, sack it, it's not worth it. I'll lower you."

"Hang on wait…. Maybe…."

"Don't risk it!"

"Sod it, let's have a go – if they attack, I'll pop the skyhook and drop. Give me loads of slack!"

I reeled out a load of rope and held my breath as I heard the noise of the drill, but within seconds Mikey let out a cry and came hurtling downwards, drill still in hand. I caught him after about 30 feet, but immediately continued lowering him, at a pace not much less than the fall itself. A small black cloud descended after him but then seemed to dissipate. We sprinted back from the crag – ropes, clutter and all – until we realized that we were no longer being chased. Mikey's eyelid had completely closed after a target hit, but I managed to suck the sting out before it got any worse.

"All yours, Neil. Over to you!"

The obvious choice was to forget the whole stupid notion, but that night, back at our favourite bar in Viñales, I just couldn't stop thinking about how amazing it would be to free-climb that incredible wave. Were the nightly "Cuba Libre"

© MIKE ROBERTSON

highballs clouding my judgment or was I really serious about going back there? The next day I gathered together every piece of protective clothing we owned and returned to sweat it out in the full sun to finish the bolting. I then removed my protective suit for long enough to make it halfway up the wall as far as the giant stalactite and *The Wasp Factory* (7b+) was born. A dream pitch in it's own right, and yet the big challenge was still on the table. So a few days later I returned to free the entire line, all the way to the top. I've climbed my share of routes with a sting in the tail but *The Colony* (8a+) took it to a different level!

There was no hanging around and celebrating at the belay this time – once again, the bars in Viñales would have to do! I'm not sure where the partying stopped and the climbing began in Cuba. The whole thing just seemed to merge together into one long crazy, hazy adventure.

Neil Gresham - Sheffield, England, 2009

CUEVA CABEZA DE LA VACA

Cueva Cabeza de la Vaca – The Cow's Head Cave – is the name of the cave/tunnel that crosses through the mogote from Raúl's farm to Vega de Pelón. On Raúl's side, the entrance forms a beautiful 30-metre overhanging wall that has become Viñales' most popular crag. It's interesting to note that the cave entrance was enlarged with explosives; the floor was flattened and a stairway was built to facilitate access for farmers and hikers who use the tunnel as a shortcut to get to the other side of the valley.

Climbers bolted the first routes here in 2000. Since then, a combination of local and foreign effort has turned this cliff into a mandatory stop for any visitor. "La Cueva", as locals call it, is the Viñales gym. In the afternoons, you can be sure to find the *Viñaleros* (locals) yo-yoing laps on *Malanga Hasta la Muerte* or trying some of the harder projects on the ferocious *Wasp Factory* overhang. The sun stays on the wall for the entire morning, so it is better to climb at this cliff after 3:00 PM. Most climbers tend to head to the other side – Vega de Pelón – in the morning, wait for the shade and then come back to Cabeza de la Vaca in the afternoon. The routes on the *Wasp Factory* overhang (the far left side) are the first ones to go into the shade.

Warming Up *Bouldering on blocks below the cave. The gold-streaked Milenio wall is in the distance.*

© MIKE ROBERTSON

The Colony (8a+) *Rob Pizem strains for a clip on this classic, stalactite-covered cave route.*

APPROACH

From Raúl's house, you can clearly see the gaping alcove of the wall and the stairs that lead from the boulder field up to the cave entrance. To reach the stairs, there are two options depending on time of year and conditions. The first follows a dirt trail that goes directly from Raúl's house to the boulder field. This path crosses between two ponds, goes over the fence using ladders and continues through the pastures to the start of the stairs behind the biggest boulder. The second option is to follow the main trail toward Ensenada de Raúl and then turn right after the gate. Please keep the gate closed and beware of the loose animals. That cute mother pig with her piglets can get pretty ugly if disturbed! Total walking time from Viñales is about 25 minutes.

THE CLIMBING

Cabeza de la Vaca has some of the best lines in Viñales and the hardest routes in Cuba. In general, the climbing is steep and physical, utilizing the plethora of tufas and stalactites dripping from the walls. Expect to get pumped; the big holds and tangled features will test your stamina and capacity to think "tridimensionally" (a word invented to refer to Cuba climbing). The hard-core endurance-fests may be the big draw here, but it's worth noting that Cabeza de la Vaca has some nice moderates and a couple of *really* easy climbs for those new to the sport. This cliff can and should be enjoyed by all.

All the routes are bolted and the rock is solid, but remember that the secondary formations (stalactites and tufas) should always be considered suspicious. Belayers, in particular, should be aware of possible rock fall, especially when standing directly under a free-hanging stalactite. The first pitches on the cliff are, by far, the most popular, but many of the routes have second pitches of equal or greater quality. With a 70-metre rope and a few long slings, it's possible to link most two-pitch routes into a single climb and still get lowered to the ground.

Note: Cueva Cabeza de la Vaca receives a large number of visitors every day. The tunnel provides access to *vegas* (tobacco fields) for farmers, facilitates school children going on field trips and allows tourists to explore the mogote, with or without a guide. Not everyone is a climber and not everyone understands climbing. Therefore, please mind the hikers walking below, avoid overcrowding, share the passage with everyone and leave the area cleaner than you found it, no matter what you see other people do. These efforts will help keep this crag open!

Cueva Cabeza de la Vaca Images *Clockwise from left: Approaching the cliff through Raúl's Farm; steep action at the tunnel entrance; the passage through to the other side; lowering off* Malanga Hasta la Muerte.

The Stairs

The first three routes are listed as you find them when approaching up the stairs.

❶ Guajiros 6b+ ★★★ . . . . ☐

This line features sustained climbing on good pockets. It goes up the left side of the orange wall that you find midway up the stairs (56 steps from the top). Start at the concrete landing at the base of a narrow patch of clean rock and climb toward the small palm tree. Sling it as protection (the first bolt always seems to be missing) and keep clipping bolts to the top. Watch the sharp rock while lowering.

1 pitch (30 M), 11 bolts *FA: Scott Cole & Armando Menocal, 2000.*

❷ Guajiras 6b ★★★★ . . . . ☐

Use the same start as the previous route, but move right after slinging the palm tree. Finish at an independent anchor.

1 pitch (31 M), bolts *FA: David Brasco, 2001.*

❸ La Cuchillita 6a ★★★ . . . . ☐

This climb starts on a concrete landing, 33 steps from the top of the stairs. To landmark the start, locate the first brown hanger about four metres from the ground, above the patch of clean rock. This routes has bolts, but requires supplemental protection. Bring some cams.

pitch 1 (4+, 25 M, 4 bolts) This pitch is a popular beginner's route. The belay station is on a ledge.

pitch 2 (6a, 26 M, 6 bolts) Climb the arête to the right and then move back left (the crux). Camalots 2–3 protect the top section. Descend with one 30-metre rappel.

2 pitches, mixed *FA: David Ryan & Armando Menocal, 2000.*

❹ Juegos de Niños 5+ ★★★ . . . . ☐

Same start as *La Cuchillita*, but climb along a line of bolts on the right.

1 pitch (25 M), 7 bolts *FA: Josué Millo.*

Tunnel Entrace

The next routes all share the same anchor, the original anchors of Malanga Hasta La Muerte *and they all climb the overhangs at the entrance of the cave. Most of the lines are independent until they meet at the roof exit or top anchors. These are some of the most climbed grade 7 routes in Viñales.*

❺ Jineteras a lo Suyo 7c ★★★★ . . . . ☐

This route starts on the right side of the cave entrance. From the last step of the stairs walk right along the low concrete bench until you reach the wall and look for the first bolts above your head. Climb the overhanging groove and move right (crux). Sustained moves all the way to the top.

1 pitch (15 M), 9 bolts *FA: Martin Molin & Ariel Pasqualeitti.*

❻ Malanga
Hasta la Muerte 7b+ ★★★★★ . . . . ☐

This is the original route inside the cave entrance. It is exceedingly popular and a superb steep limestone cave climb. It starts on buckets on the right side of the cave and reaches the first bolt at five metres – get your belayer to spot you! It then traverses across the roof and exits above the cave entrance. The crux is finding the best features in the confusing matrix of horizontal rock. With imagination, you will find great rests: knee bars, full-body stems and shoulder wedges! The route is so steep that someone must toprope it to clean the draws. Please note that the belayer should be very careful with the amount of slack when the climber is above the entrance boulder.

1 pitch (15 M), 9 bolts *FA: David Brasco & Rosa Catalá, 2001.*

stairs
CABEZA DE LA VACA RIGHT

7 Otra Mano "Pa" el Pulpo 7c ★★★ ☐

This is a harder, three bolt start for *Malanga* that can cause confusion because the bolts are on the harder looking section between *Malanga* and *Jineteras*. The name translates to "another hand for the octopus". In other words, it's another limb for *Malanga*.
1 pitch (15 M), 9 bolts *FA: Josué Millo & Reiniel Sosa, 2005.*

8 Tiburones Viñaleros 7c ★★★★ .... ☐

This route climbs the longest roof section. It starts from the top of the cement box and climbs the roof to where a junction with *Malanga* at the exit. Sustained on big holds.
1 pitch (20 M) 11 bolts *FA: Ned Harris & Alberto Leivas, 2002.*

9 ¡Misericordia por Dios! 7b ★★★★ ☐

This line starts on the left side, just inside the cave and has a bouldery crux.
1 pitch (15 M), 9 bolts *FA: Josué Millo & Reiniel Sosa, 2005.*

Tunnel Routes Left

The following routes spurn the obvious upward direction of all the Cueva's other lines by climbing back into the cave, ending in almost total darkness (a headlamp may even help locate the anchors). The routes are listed from left to right on the left wall, as you enter the cave.

10 Camino al Infierno 7a ★★ .... ☐

This climb starts from the top, right edge of the cement box and heads into the cave, generally staying on the left side of the roof. This and the next four routes climb from the left side of the cave along the roof toward the rear of the cave.
1 pitch (15 M), 7 bolts *FA: Josué Millo & Alberto Leivas, 2005.*

11 Los Tres Mosqueteros 7b ★★ .... ☐

The first route on the left, *inside* the cave.
1 pitch (7 M), 3 bolts *FA: Josué Millo & Alberto Leivas, 2005.*

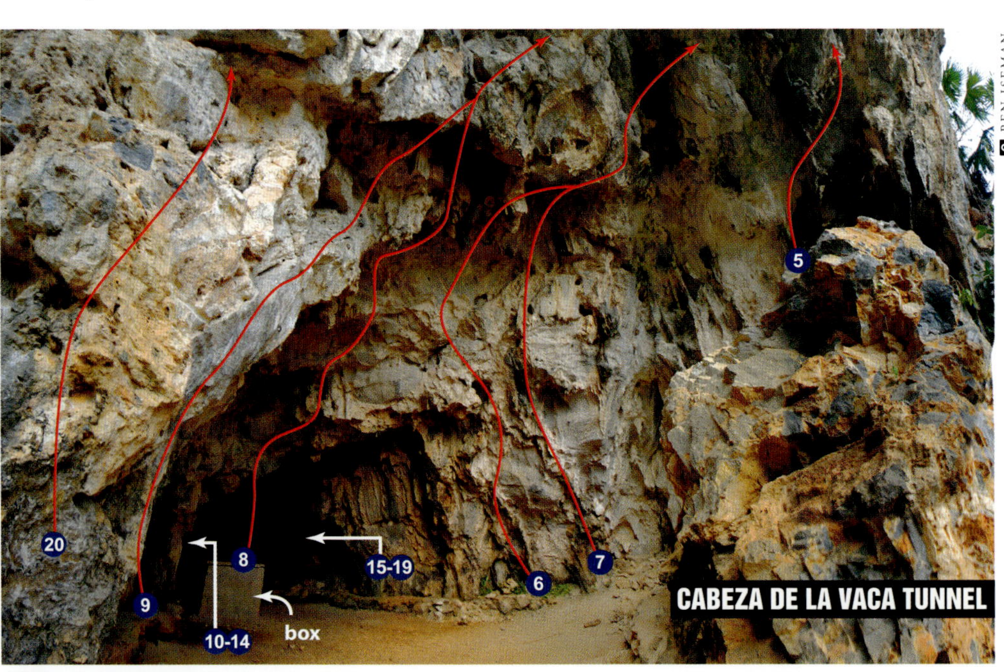

⑫ Na Pa Nadie Pa 7b+ ★★ . . . . ☐

Just right of *Los Tres Mosqueteros.*
1 pitch (7 M), 3 bolts *FA: Josué Millo & Alberto Leivas, 2005.*

⑬ Haista 6c ★★ . . . . ☐

Start by a stalactite. Join *Golondrina* (coming from the opposite side) in the roof.
1 pitch (8 M), 3 bolts *FA: Josué Millo & Alberto Leivas, 2005.*

⑭ Candilejas 6c ★★ . . . . ☐

The last route on the left, past the stalactite.
1 pitch (8 M), 3 bolts *FA: Josué Millo, 2005.*

Tunnel Routes Right

The following five routes (Anadurina through M-1) are on the right side of the cave and, like the above climbs, move from the front to the back of the cave.

⑮ Chicharrónes 8a+ ★★ . . . . ☐

The first route on the right, *inside* the cave.
1 pitch (9 M), 4 bolts *FA: Josué Millo & Fransua Bosmenier, 2005.*

⑯ Anduriña 8a ★★ . . . . ☐

The next route to the left.
1 pitch (9 M), 3 bolts *FA: Josué Millo & Fransua Bosmenier, 2005.*

⑰ Guiro que Te Escachas 7c ★★ . . . . ☐

1 pitch (9 M), 3 bolts *FA: Josué Millo & Raiquel Reyes, 2005.*

⑱ Golondrina 6b+ ★★ . . . . ☐

Climbs by stalactites right of *M-1.*
1 pitch (9 M), 3 bolts *FA: Josué Millo & Raiquel Reyes, 2005.*

⑲ M-1 8a ★★ . . . . ☐

Look for a yellow "M-1" painted on the rock.
1 pitch (9 M), 4 bolts *FA: Josué Millo, FFA: Unknown Venezuelan climber, 2005.*

Left Overhang

The following routes are listed from right to left, beginning at the top of the stairs.

⑳ Puro Cubano 7a+ ★★★★ . . . . ☐

This was the first route in Cabeza de la Vaca and the first pitch is a popular moderate.
pitch 1 (6b+, 30 M, 7 bolts) The original route starts on top of the stairs and follows the tufas almost directly up to a crack and a ramp. Finish over a small roof (crux) to the anchors in the small cave. Most people lower from the ring-cable anchor right below the cave.
pitch 2 (3+, 17 M) From the original anchors, traverse right (walk) on the ledge behind the tufas to another anchor. Belay here.
pitch 3 (7a+, 20 M) This is a great pitch that most people pass on. Climb up and left. Descend by rappelling 30 metres to the stairs
3 pitches, bolts *FA: Vitalio Echazábal, Armando Menocal & David Ryan, 2000.*

㉑ Maya 7c ★★★★ . . . . ☐

This difficult second pitch starts at the original *Puro Cubano* anchor and goes up and left toward the white stalactite.
1 pitch (15 M), bolts *FA: Abel Pérez & Loisbel Silvelio.*

㉒ Cubanitos en la Red 6c ★★★ . . . . ☐

Start as for the first pitch *Puro Cubano*, but head right above the edge of the cave entrance.
1 pitch (20 M), bolts *FA: Josué Millo, 2002.*

㉓ Unnamed 7b ★★★ . . . . ☐

Climb up and left from the anchor on *Cubanitos en la Red.*
1 pitch (15 M), bolts *FA: Los Titos.*

㉔ Project 8a? . . . . ☐

Climb up and right from the anchor on *Cubanitos en la Red.*
1 pitch (15 M), bolts *FA: Unclimbed.*

㉕ Chao Pescao 6b+ ★★★ ....☐

A squeezed line just left of *Puro Cubanos*. The name means "goodbye fish" and is a catchy rhyme used to say goodbye in the Caribbean.
1 pitch (25 M), 6 bolts *FA: Josué Millo, 2005.*

㉖ RM 6a+ ★★★★ ....☐

This is a nice warm-up that is steep for the grade. Start at the right edge of the little alcove, just left of the tree, and climb big tufas and stalactites all the way to the upper ramp.
1 pitch (25 M), 6 bolts *FA: David Brasco and Rosa Catalá, 2001.*

㉗ Quien Dijo Miedo Habiendo Hospitales 7c ★★★★ ......☐

Start on a stalactite left of *RM*. Two fun pitches go at 6c+ and 7c.
2 pitches, bolts *FA: Josué Millo, 2002.*

㉘ Kid Expresivo 6c+ ★★★★ ....☐

Climb interesting formations on the left side of the little alcove. Clip the first bolt at the ledge and follow the crack leaning to the right. More cracks and jugs will get you past the roof crux. There are good rests.
1 pitch (27 M), 7 bolts *FA: Aníbal Fernández, 2002.*

㉙ Na Pa Pié 7c ★★★ ....☐

Start near *Kid Expresivo*, but trend up the technical wall to the left. The upper roof is 7b with a 60 metre rappel to the ground!
2 pitches, bolts *FA: Josué Millo, Alberto Leivas & Reiniel Sosa, 2002.*

㉚ A Martillazo Limpio 7a ★★★★ .....☐

Start on the cruxy face left of the alcove and climb up left to a slab, a small roof and a ledge. You can lower from here, but it is recommended to continue up the steep, cruxy wall. Bring long slings to avoid rope drag.
1 pitch (30 M), 12 bolts *FA: Josué Millo & Reiniel Sosa, 2002.*

㉛ Totisnao 6b ★★★★ ....☐

This good warm-up route is just left of *A Martillazo*. The start is similar, but easier, and is followed by a small roof and a very enjoyable overhanging dihedral. Use a sling on the bolt below the first roof to reduce rope drag.
1 pitch (25 M), 12 bolts *FA: Aníbal Fernández & Josué Millo, 2002.*

㉜ Chimeneando 6b+ ★★ ....☐

This is the original, but less natural, start of *Totisnao*. Start on a slabby section, climb the tufas in the overhang and then deke right into *Totisnao* halfway up.
1 pitch (25 M), 11 bolts *FA: Josué Millo, 2002.*

㉝ La Playa 7a ★★★★ ....☐

This route starts at a slabby section and climbs stalactites and tufas (7a, 25 M, 10 bolts). The upper roof pitches are 6c+ (left) and 7b (right). Watch the rope, as it's easy to get it tangled with the route's features.
2 pitches, bolts *FA: Mike Robertson & Anna Greissing, 2002.*

㉞ La Mierda 6b+ ....☐

La Mierda – The Shit – follows an obvious and bullish profile, but unfortunately fails as a quality route. It is dirty and the bolts are not well-located (one bolt is placed *on a stalactite*). Two alternate starts to the right have been added by Josué Millo, but they fail to add quality. His variations are also aptly named: *Papel Hijienico* and *Limpiste* (*Toilet Paper* and *Wipe Yourself*). Not recommended.
1 pitch (15 M), 6 bolts *FA: Unknown Polish Climbers.*

> **Interesting Fact:** *Malanga Hasta la Muerte follows the initial line of the first "climb" in the cave, which was called Taking the Bull by the Horns. This "route" consisted of a bizarre, five-metre toprope boulder problem.*

CABEZA DE LA VACA LEFT

35 Esplendidos 8a ★★★★★ ....□

Esplendidos starts up a rock bulge in front of the wall before forging onto the sustained overhang. It gets progressively steeper and harder, with a couple of crux moves at the bitter end. Tim Emmett said, "Totally awesome, one of the best 8a routes you'll ever do!"
1 pitch (22 M), 10 bolts *FA: Tim Emmett, 2002.*

36 One-Inch Punch 8b+ ★★★★★ .....□

This is the extension of *Esplendidos* out the vicious, final roof. It's the hardest route in Cuba and one of the best of its grade in Central America. Emmett called it, "The best route I have ever done." Neil Gresham concurred, "As good, if not better than *Punks in the Gym* or *The Rose and the Vampire*."
1 pitch (30 M), 15 bolts *FA: Tim Emmett, 2002.*

37 The Wasp Factory 7b+ ★★★★★ ...□

This route is another work of art. Start just left of the rock bulge and follow a striking line of small tufas to finish on top of the massive, hanging stalactite. This is a must-do staminafest for anyone with the right stuff.
1 pitch (25 M), 9 bolts *FA: Neil Gresham, 2002.*

38 The Colony 8a+ ★★★★★ ....□

The natural extension of *The Wasp Factory* forges out the final roof. The entire link-up is 35 metres and has a desperate boulder problem in the final section, just where you least want it.
1 pitch (35 M), 15 bolts *FA: Neil Gresham, 2002.*

39 Morirse a Plazo 8a ★★ ....□

Start beside *The Wasp Factory* and finish on the left side of the massive stalactite.
1 pitch (20 M), 9 bolts *FA: Josué Millo, Yarobys García & Alberto Leiva, 2006.*

40 Echando Candela 8a ★★ ....□

Climb direct into *Morirse a Plazo*.
1 pitch (20 M), 8 bolts *FA: Josué Millo, Yarobys García & Alberto Leiva, 2006.*

41 Virosis 7b+ ★★ ....□

Climb to the left of the column. Join *Saca Chispas* near the top.
1 pitch (15 M), 8 bolts *FA: Josué Millo, Yarobys García & Alberto Leiva, 2006.*

42 Saca Chispas 7a+ ★★★★ ....□

Climb pockets, tufas and huecos to an overhanging layback using a left-facing crack. You'll find a bouldery move after the third bolt.
1 pitch (15 M), 9 bolts *FA: Josué Millo & Yarobys García, 2002.*

43 Vamo Allá 6c ★★★ ....□

Face climbing leads to some small stalactites.
1 pitch (18 M), 9 bolts *FA: Yarobys García & Maikel Novo, 2007.*

44 Rosca Izquierda 6c ★★ ....□

The far left line on the main wall.
1 pitch (20 M), bolts *FA: Alberto Leiva, 2007.*

Piedra Mi Cusi

Three short routes on the small buttress.

45 Feliz Cumpleaños 6a ★★ ....□

Climb the right-hand line on the small face.
1 pitch (13 M), 5 bolts *FA: Alberto Leiva, 2007.*

46 Mi Cusi 5+ ★★ ....□

This is a popular novice route because you can walk to the top of the boulder and set a toprope without needing to lead. The route climbs the centre of the boulder.
1 pitch (15 M), 7 bolts *FA: Josué Millo, 2004.*

47 Cara Dura 6a ★★ ....□

Start down and left from the previous route. Climb a harder line with some sharp holds to the same anchor as *Mi Cusi*.
1 pitch (15 M), 6 bolts *FA: Josué Millo, 2004.*

The Wasp Factory (7b+) *Naomi Guy comes to grips with some Cuban stalactites.*

PAREDÓN DE JOSUÉ

Vega de Pelón is a quiet, cultivated farming valley that has a nice selection of crags with a good variety of routes, including some quality novice lines. Thus far, three of the walls encircling the valley have been developed, but the most of the routes, by far, are on the Paredón de Josué. The name of this cliff is a nod to Josué Millo, who developed 15 of the 17 established climbs on the wall. Paredón de Josué is shaded from early morning onward, making it a cool refuge from the heat. The upper section of the crag is often breezy, which also adds to the comfort quotient.

APPROACH

Most people reach this crag by walking through the tunnel at Cabeza de la Vaca. You don't need a light to pass through the tunnel, except perhaps at night. The floor has been leveled and light can be seen at the far end just as the entrance fades to black. Once at the Vega de Pelón side, follow a steep trail down into the valley. Upon reaching the flats, Paredón de Josué is about 50 metres ahead on the left. Since you approach this wall through a farmer's field, please be careful not to damage any crops. Once at the cliff, the trail goes left to some short routes and right for the main wall. Total walking time from Viñales is about 30 minutes.

THE CLIMBING

The climbing at Paredón de Josué is not nearly as steep as in Cabeza de la Vaca. Instead, the cliff has long sections of vertical and gently overhanging rock laced various cracks and smallish tufas. There are short routes on the left side, but on the right the pitches are a full 30 metres.

Vega de Pelón *The views of the farm from the north side of the tunnel are stunning and highlight the lushness of the surroundings.*

Paredón de Josué

Routes are listed from left to right.

① Calentando Baterías 6a ★★★★ ... ☐

This is a good warm-up. It starts on the far left, close to the Jaguey tree, and climbs the grey face and the corner above. The anchor is a bit to the right and is shared with the next route.

1 pitch (20 M), 6 bolts *FA: Josué Millo & Yarobys García, 2002.*

② Chan Chan de Ilusiones 6c ★★★★★ .... ☐

This routes starts on the crack, but moves left after the third bolt to reach the anchors of *Calentando Baterias*. It's a very nice climb; footwork is the key on the traverse.

1 pitch (20 M), 7 bolts *FA: Yarobys García & Josué Millo, 2002.*

③ Tarentola 6a+ ★★★★ .... ☐

This is the original line that follows the diagonal crack to the ledge and finishes on top of the wide crack. It's a popular moderate.

1 pitch (25 M), 8 bolts *FA: Aníbal Fernández & Josué Millo, 2002.*

④ Romeo y Regleta 7b+ ★★★★★ .... ☐

This route climbs the face between the two cracks and joins *Tarentola* at the ledge. It has a very delicate crux on small holds. This is a challenging route and a local classic.

1 pitch (25 M), 8 bolts *FA: Aníbal Fernández & Josué Millo, 2002.*

⑤ Guajiro Natural 6b+ ★★★★ ...... ☐

This is the crack in front of you when you reach the base of the wall from the trail. A bouldery move gains the initial tufa pinch.

1 pitch (25 M), 8 bolts *FA: Aníbal Fernández & Josué Millo, 2002.*

6 Por la Raja de Tu Falda 6c ★★ . . . . ☐

This line tackles the next crack, starting from the boulder. Unfortunately, it's a bit dirty, at least for the moment.

1 pitch (25 M), 7 bolts *FA: Josué Millo & Yunieszy Gonzales, 2002.*

7 Economizando Baterias 6b ★★ . . . ☐

Use the first bolt (of the two on top of the boulder) to move left and up to the in-situ thread on the big stalactite. Mind the quality of the thread and add your own if you can. Double shoulder slings will do.

1 pitch (25 M), bolts *FA: Reinier Sosa & Josué Millo, 2002.*

8 Reversible 6b+ ★★★ . . . . ☐

This route takes the same start as the previous one, but follows the line of the second bolt off the boulder. Climb the left side of the big stalactite column. The upper section offers a choice: left of the bolts is 6a and to the right side is 6c. Pick your line.

1 pitch (25 M), bolts *FA: Josué Millo & Raikel Reyes, 2002.*

9 Mujer, Peligro y Placer 6b+ ★★★★ ☐

This pitch starts up right side of the column.

1 pitch (20 M), bolts *FA: Josué Millo & Yuniesky Gonzales, 2002.*

10 Mancha en Mi Expediente 8a ★★★ ☐

The route climbs the roof right of the big column. This route has the only manufactured hand hold in Viñales.

1 pitch (30 M), bolts *FA: Josué Millo & Yuniesky Gonzales, 2002.*

11 Pies de Homo Hábilis 7b ★★★★ . . . ☐

Start on the boulders and climb a vertical crack to the roof. Follow the diagonal line to the left through the roof crux and keep going up the face toward a second overhang.

1 pitch (30 M), 12 bolts *FA: Josué Millo, 2002.*

12 Dame Luz San Valentín 7a ★★★★ ☐

This climb is very close to the previous route, but follows a more direct path up to the same anchors. Start on the diagonal crack.

1 pitch (30 M), 11 bolts *FA: Josué Millo & Alberto Leivas, 2002.*

13 Melodía Celestial 6c ★★★★★ . . . . . ☐

Start over the right boulder and gun for the right-facing crack. Be careful not to fall and deck clipping the third bolt! This is a very nice climb, but has a sharp finish.

1 pitch (30 M), 12 bolts *FA: Alberto Leivas & Josué Millo, 2002.*

14 Terapia de Miedo 7a+ ★★★★ . . . . . ☐

This route climbs a wide arête right of *Melodia Celestial*. Clipping the first bolt is tricky. Get a spot or use a stick-clip.

1 pitch (30 M), 12 bolts *FA: Josué Millo & Raikel Reyes, 2002.*

15 Cuando los Ángeles lloran 7a ★★★★★ . . . . ☐

Start to the right of the boulder.

1 pitch (30 M), 12 bolts *FA: Yarobys García & Alberto Leivas, 2007.*

16 Rebentadera 6b ★★★ . . . . ☐

The route is apparently unfinished, but you can climb it using the anchors from the previous route. Start very close to the vegetation.

1 pitch (30 M), 11 bolts *FA: Alberto Leivas, 2007.*

17 Sorpresa 6b ★★★★ . . . . ☐

This is a good route that you will find if you walk 50 metres right of the previous routes. When you see a wide crack, you're there.

pitch 1 (6b, 30 M) Climb the orange wall.

pitch 2 (6a+, 30 M) Continue up past the small cave.

2 pitches, bolts *FA: Josué Millo & Raikel Reyes, 2002.*

PAREDÓN DE JOSUÉ

JARUQUIÑO

Like Paredón de Josué, this crag on the other side of Cueva Cabeza de la Vaca, however it might need a bit more development and traffic to become as popular. Since most people head to the Vega de Pelón to climb at Paredón the Josué, you can find peace and solitude at this cliff, if you so desire. Jaruquiño has three interesting routes that are permanently shaded.

APPROACH

Approach as for Paredón de Josué, through the Cabeza de la Vaca tunnel and down into the valley. Jaruquiño is the white, north-facing wall to the right of the trail and the view improves as you continue walking north. After about 50 metres, turn right across the fields and look for a small trail behind the trees. Hike over boulders to the base of the first route, which is at the right end of the crag. This approach is about a 35-minute walk from Viñales.

THE CLIMBING

This cliff hosts three obvious, moderate lines, all with very different characteristics.

View from tunnel

Jaruquiño

Routes are listed from right to left.

❶ Titos 6c ★★★★ . . . . ☐

This is the first line you reach when approaching the crag. It starts on conglomerate and follows the overhanging face covered with small tufas. They look fragile, but you'll be surprised!
1 pitch (15 M), bolts *FA: The Pimentel Brothers.*

❷ Nicotina 5 ★★ . . . . ☐

Keep moving left along the bouldery and steep base to find this wide crack that becomes a fully-overhanging chimney higher up.
1 pitch (20 M), bolts *FA: Aníbal Fernández & José Luís Gómez, 2005.*

❸ Escabiosis 6c+ ★★★ . . . . ☐

This route starts a bit higher up on top of a boulder. Climb the diagonal crack, move left at the ledge and then up the blocky section. The top overhang with tree roots is the crux.
1 pitch (25 M), bolts *FA: Aníbal Fernández & José Luís Gómez, 2005.*

View from fields

SECTOR GEISHA

Sector Geisha is another small, shady crag on the north side of Mogote del Valle. It has a couple of good climbs on sound rock. The name of the crag was inspired by the Geisha-like look of the developer after drilling the routes: his body and face were plastered in white rock dust.

APPROACH

Follow the trail past Paredón de Josué and along the fields until you reach the corner of the mogote. Sector Geisha is the small overhanging wall on the left, at the level of the crops. This approach is about a 35-minute walk from Viñales.

THE CLIMBING

Each route is steep with a diversity of movement.

Sector Geisha

Routes are listed from left to right.

❶ Pichulina San 7b+ ★★★★★ ..☐

This excellent climb requires a wide range of techniques. Start on the cracks and then continue up to the steepest part of the wall. The pitch is sustained with a crux at the top.
1 pitch (18 M), bolts *FA: Aníbal Fernández & Abel Pérez, 2005.*

❷ Shogun 6b ★★★★ ....☐

The easiest line climbs to big ledges on the right. It finishes up the dihedral.
1 pitch (20 M), bolts *FA: Abel Pérez & Aníbal Fernández, 2005.*

"Why climb?" Responses to this question are incredibly varied and I don't have a clear answer, but I can tell you why climbing is important to me, and how it entered my life. It all started when I was 13 years old and picked up the colourful coffee table book *Rocks Around the World*. The pages bulged with pictures of climbers clinging to crazy overhanging rocks and doing amazing moves on steep, exposed cliffs – I was hooked.

Living in Cuba, the possibility for real climbing adventures seemed distant, but I wanted to learn more. I read all the climbing-related stories I could find, and the accounts portrayed a type of adventure that really captivated me. The carefree climbers in the pictures seemed detached from reality, yet in harmony with everything around them and that was seductive. Maybe it was the tight spandex, but it looked like a dance to me – a type of dance that I thought I would like!

Climbing in Cuba? People actually cringed when I started asking around. Climbing was associated with alpinism, and the mountains in Cuba had no snow! The whole idea seemed absurd, but I was enough of a rebel to push forward and ignore the naysayers. I knew I only needed two things to get started: a good cliff and a dangling rope! The walls were there, I had seen them on my camping trips, but I had absolutely no idea how to get the rope up.

My learning process started by cutting the seat belts out of my dad's Lada and improvising harnesses for myself and a couple of unsuspecting buddies. Some local cavers taught us to rappel and ascend ropes but, unfortunately, none of them seemed to know anything about real rock climbing. We managed to buy some of their muddy ropes, but had to conduct our own "in-depth research" into proper climbing technique… by reading a Petzl catalogue! Incredibly, we figured out how to set up topropes and belay with a *homemade* figure eight device. We survived, and from this point forward things just got better and better. We frequently travelled to random cliffs to set up topropes and did laps until our fingers bled. Eventually, we started using caving bolts, pitons and homemade chocks, which allowed us to lead our first routes. These experiments, combined with some bouldering, a few more books, and a ton of good fortune, got us through our initial learning period – my first barefoot years that made me fall in love with the sport for life!

I won't bore you with the entire story of how we actually learned to climb and managed to survive, and I'll spare you the details of the economical, social and political hurdles that we had to overcome. Although I'd like to mention all the good friends that were part of this incredible journey, I won't for fear I'll forget someone. But like every Cuban story, ours is loaded with passion, laughs, tears, blood, scars, friends, enemies, misunderstandings, exile, rhythm and romance. I find the retelling of these stories tedious and I'd much rather leave you with the end result of our adventures – the incredible rock climbing in Cuba, our dream fulfilled.

Aníbal Fernández - Canada, 2009

Sierra de Guasasa *Lots of virgin rock lies to the north of Mogote Palmarito.*

CHAPTER 3

MOGOTE PALMARITO

Mogote Palmarito is a small, pincusion hill located directly north of the eastern tip of the much larger Mogote del Valle. This crag is actually quite close to Viñales – about a two-kilometre walk – and is readily visible when travelling north from town. The name is derived from the small neighbourhood of houses nested below the mogote – the community of Palmarito.

Despite having only a few short, moderate climbs, this mogote is still worth a visit. The cliff has a true summit – a rarity in Viñales – and is conveniently located close to the road that runs between Viñales and El Palenque. Check it out.

MOGOTE PALMARITO

APPROACH

Head north out of Viñales and look for the low mogote on the west (left) side of the road. It is visible just before you reach the paved right turnoff to Mogote de los Hoyos or the unpaved left turnoff to the neighborhood of Palmarito. Mogote Palmarito has a free-standing pinnacle on its south that can be seen from the road and there is a dirt road that provides access to the fields adjacent to the pinnacle. The approach takes about five minutes from the parking area.

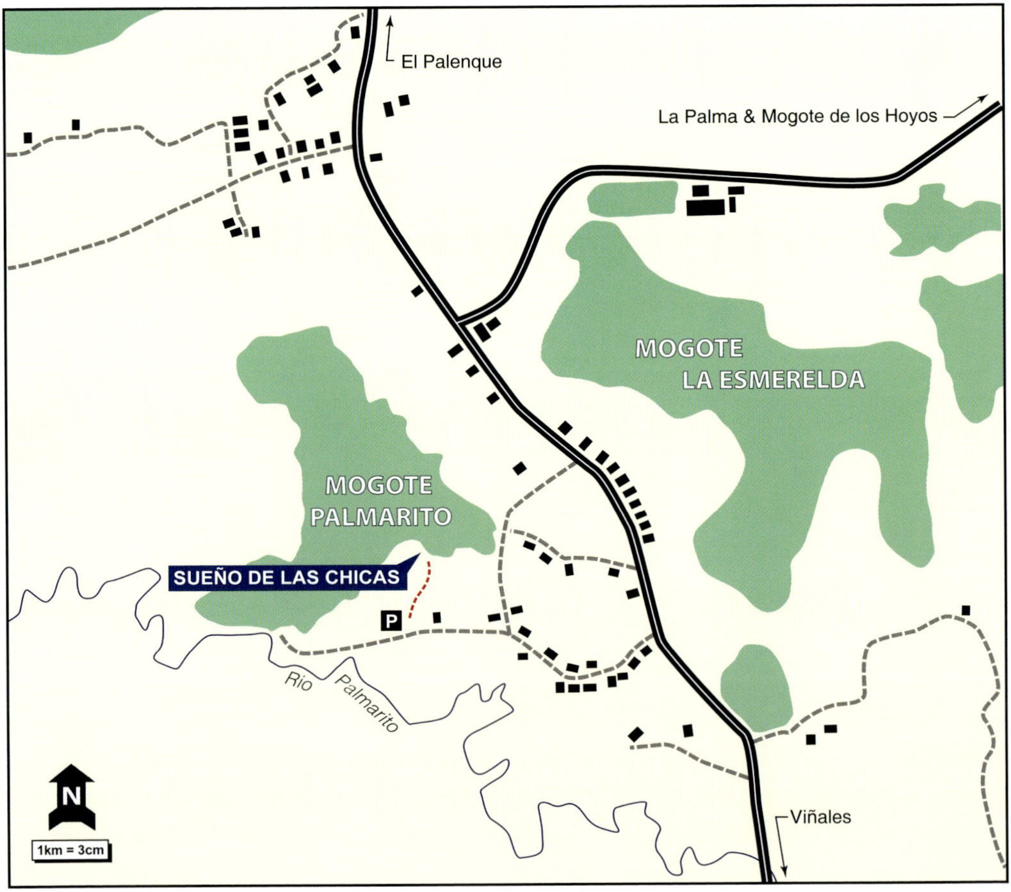

CLIMBING

The routes here are short and easy on a small feature in the middle of the farms and *bohios* (traditional thatched rural homes). Unfortunately, little is know about these climbs, hence the lack of quality ratings.

Mogote Palmarito

Routes are listed from left to right (no topo).

❶ Sueño de las Chicas 6a . . . . ☐

Looking from the south, the prominent feature of the pinnacle is a large hole partway up. This route starts two metres left of the hole. Bring seven quickdraws.

1 pitch (20 M), 7 bolts *FA: Paul Laperrière, 2002.*

❷ Zero Positivo 6a+ . . . . ☐

Starts from the hole.

1 pitch (20 M), 7 bolts *FA: Markus Leicht, 2002.*

❸ Moneando 5 . . . . ☐

This climb starts up a tree and uses the top bolts of *Sueno de las Chicas*. Some threads supplement the bolts.

1 pitch (25 M), bolts *FA: Josué Millo, 2002.*

Farmland *A traditional barn, often used for drying tobacco, sits in the fields behind a "ceiba" tree.*

CHAPTER 4

PALENQUE AREA

The Palenque Area offers high quality climbing on a variety of unique crags, well worth the short taxi ride from Viñales. In particular, the pocket caves of Cuba Libre Wall are exceptional and contain some very steep, stalactite-studded roofs that have to be seen to be believed. All of the climbs in this sector are in the *abra* (pass) between the Sierra de Viñales and Sierra de Guasasa, two of the biggest formations of mogotes.

A unique aspect to visiting this zone is El Palenque, a restaurant/disco built directly into the San Miguel caves. For the first foreign and Cuban climbers, El Palenque was perhaps the most indulgent base-camp in all of climbing. The bar provided the crew with rest and refreshments after a strenuous day of route building, and many new climbs were named for the disco songs that wafted out over the fields. Those days have passed, but El Palenque still offers an interesting diversion and après-climbing hangout for travellers spending a day cragging in this zone.

© BETH WALD (LYNN HILL ON CAPTAIN HOOK)

PALENQUE AREA APPROACH

To access the crags at El Palenque, you need to take the highway north out of Viñales toward Puerto Esperanza. About four kilometres north of town, the road curves between the impressive wall of Mr. Mogote on the right and the stalactite-covered overhangs of Cuba Libre on the left. The El Palenque entrance and parking lot are signed, just on the other side of the small divide.

Note: Please keep a low profile in the parking area and at the Cuba Libre trailhead to minimize friction with the owners of El Palenque. Also, please be careful not to trample crops when crossing the fields to Palenque Wall.

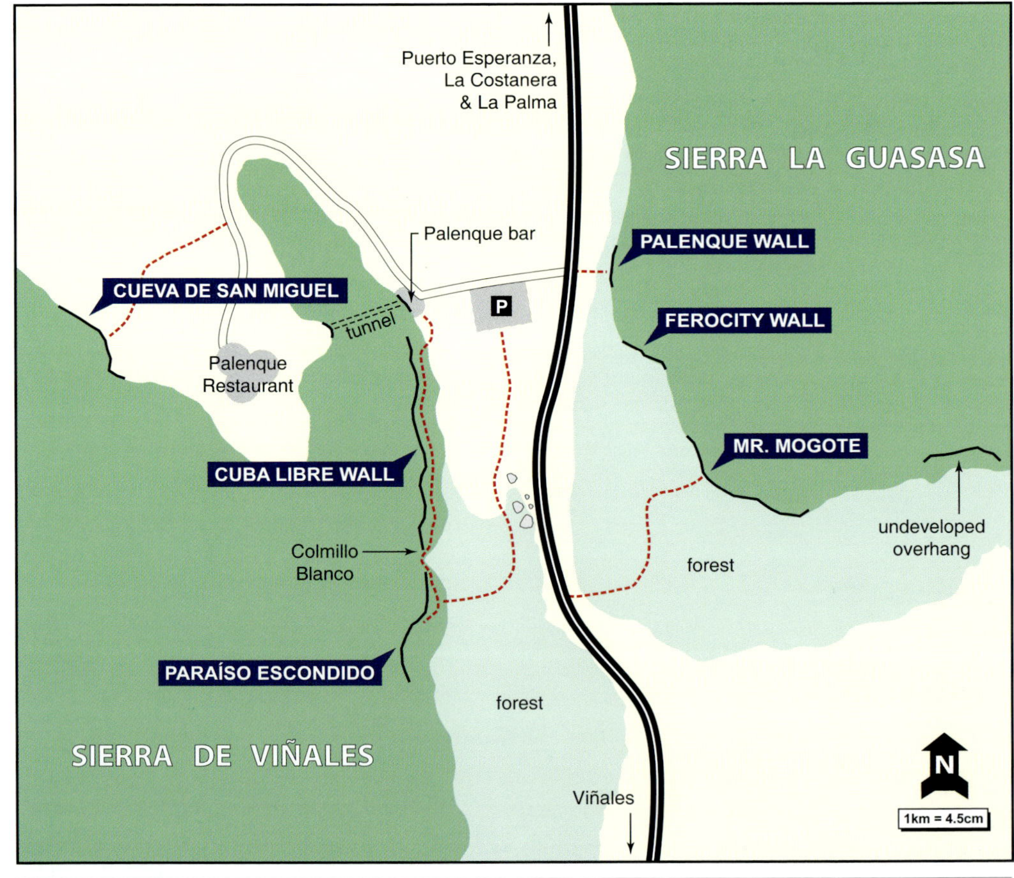

Fertile Fields *Farming is very common in the lush valleys between Viñales' mogotes. The red earth is rich in minerals and the warm, moist climate provides an ideal environment for many crops to grow including tobacco, coffee, rice, corn and various types of tropical fruit. Palenque Wall is adjacent to a farm; please tread gently when approaching.*

Cueva de San Miguel *Runaway slaves once hid in the depths of this cave, but today tourists congregate to eat in the El Palenque restaurant and enjoy evening shows at the disco/bar.*

Local Transportation *Traditional horse carriages are common at Cuban resorts such as Veradero and are government run, but privately owned horse carts are common along fixed routes in the small villages and are a pleasant change from a taxi-assisted approach to the cliff.*

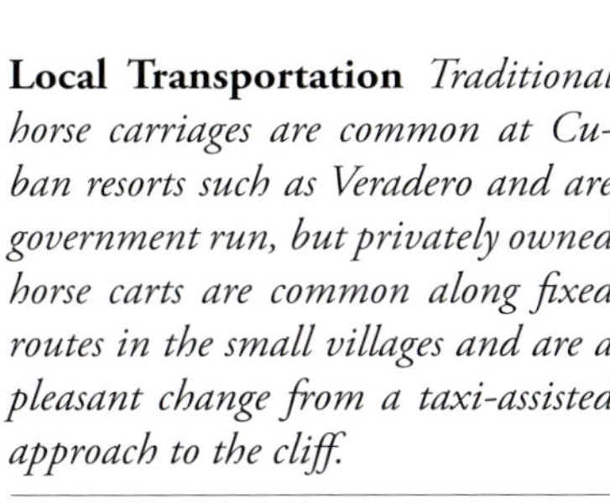

PALENQUE WALL

Palenque Wall is part of the Sierra La Guasasa and is located just off the road, across from the Cuba Libre caves. This nice crag was the first to be fully developed in Viñales and likely in all of Cuba. In 1999, a team of American climbers prepared four bolted lines and one traditional route on the wall. A year later, the Spaniards added an additional line and the cliff was complete. For climbers visiting today, note that this wall gets quite a bit of sun so it's better if you climb in the late afternoon or on cloudy days.

APPROACH

This crag is directly across the road from the entrance and parking area for El Palenque bar and is partially hidden by the trees. It takes about five minutes to approach and you will need to jump a fence and cross a small field. Be careful with the crops, please.

THE CLIMBING

This cliff features very solid rock that offers a combination of crack and face climbing. It is slightly overhanging and spiced with the occasional small tufa. Palenque Wall is a good introduction to the area before tackling the more disorienting world of mega-stalactites across the street at Cuba Libre! The longest route is 30 metres and the start of some lines is a tad runout, but on easy terrain.

Mr. Nice (7c) *The beautiful orange-streaked Ferocity Wall is just uphill of Palenque Wall.*

Palenque Wall

This wall is located directly across the road from the parking lot for El Palenque bar. Routes are listed from left to right.

❶ ¡Socialismo o Muerte! 6a ★★★★ ..☐

This is a good warm-up. Start climbing on the lower angle section on the far left end of the base and finish in a small cave.

1 pitch (25 M), 11 bolts *FA: Armando Menocal, Skip Harper & George Bracksieck, 1999.*

❷ Confiscado 6c ★★★★★ ....☐

This is the second bolted line that climbs the overhanging face above the first ledge. The top part joins the previous route.

1 pitch (25 M), 11 bolts *FA: Craig Luebben & George Bracksieck, 1999.*

❸ ¡Allez, Allez, Allez! 6b+ ★★★★★ ...☐

Climb up to the ledge using the first bolt of *Confiscado*. Follow the crack to the right and then up the steeper section. You might want to protect the crack with a large cam or hex. A

climber fractured her skull falling off this part of the route with the rope behind her legs!

1 pitch (23 M), 8 bolts *FA: Craig Luebben, 1999.*

❹ La Kirenia 6c ★★★★★ ....☐

Use *Confiscado's* first bolts to protect your way to the ledge before traversing right to the line of golden hangers. Some just run it out to the first bolt.

1 pitch (30 M), 12 bolts *FA: Javier Alvarez & Carlos Pinelo, 1999.*

❺ Mi Amore 6b ★★★★ ....☐

Start right of the fallen tree. The first eight metres need to be protected with gear or climbed with extreme caution.

1 pitch (22 M), 4 bolts *FA: Craig Leubben, 1999.*

❻ Clásica 6a+ ★★★ ....☐

The last route on the right edge of the wall is climbed using gear, but finishes at a bolted station. The moves involve pulling on roots; it's seldom climbed. Bring nuts and cams to 4 inches.

1 pitch (22 M), gear *FA: Craig Luebben, 1999.*

Ferocity Wall

This is the pretty, orange-streaked wall up the hill from Palenque Wall. Currently, there is only one route. The base is about a 10-minute walk from the road and is accessed via a rightward traverse from the bottom of Palenque Wall.

❼ Mr. Nice 7c ★★★ ....☐

Climb straight up to the diagonal break and then move left to a large ledge. Move to the left-hand end and then climb the groove above to an obvious pocket. Continue straight up the wall on small crimps to a hard rock-over (crux) and the belay. A long quickdraw on the fourth bolt helps reduce rope drag.

1 pitch (30 M), 10 bolts *FA: Charlie Woodburn, 2002.*

YAROBYS GARCÍA

PALENQUE WALL

MR. MOGOTE WALL

Mr. Mogote wall is on the east side of Abra de Ancón (the pass) when travelling north from Viñales. It's a large, imposing cliff, laced with caverns, stalactites and cacti. Currently, it sports a lone five-pitch climb, but the potential for more development is significant. This wall is home to one of the bivy caves – Casa Gringo – that climbers who *insist* on camping often use. The developers spent only a few nights in Casa Gringo.

APPROACH

Near the high point of the pass, look for a trail that heads uphill toward the crag. It's about a 15-minute hike to the wall.

THE CLIMBING

Craig Luebben became obsessed with this route and devoted two climbing trips from the United States to establishing it. Luebben's determination in leading the second pitch – with machete and drill, chopping through cactus and barbed aloe plants – was infamous and earned him the nickname "Mr. Mogote", by the locals. The route is full-value and features all kinds of climbing from technical face moves to steep tufa pulling. The first two pitches aren't spectacular, but the last three are, so don't get discouraged!

1 **Mr. Mogote 7a+** ★★★★ . . . . ☐

This is one of the longest climbs in Viñales.

pitch 1: "Donde Esta La Guagua?" (7a+, 25 M, 8 bolts) Climb the clean, overhanging strip.

pitch 2: "Aloe Highway" (5, 20 M, 3 bolts) Scramble left from the anchors and then climb over a vertical section. Walk to the white wall and the anchors.

pitch 3: "White Wall" (6c+, 30 M, 10 bolts) Technical face climbing on small holds.

pitch 4: "Tufa Paradise" (7a+, 30 M, 12 bolts) Navigate tufas in an exposed position.

pitch 5: "Mr. Magoo Meets Mr. Mogote" (6b+, 30 M, 8 bolts) Easier, but spectacular!

Descent: Lower or rappel to the pitch 4 anchors. From here, a 60 metre rappel reaches the base of the white wall. Walk right under the black overhangs to Casa Gringo. A rappel anchor faces Viñales; 50 metres to the base.

5 pitches, mixed *FA: Craig Luebben & Cameron Cross, 1999.*

MR. MOGOTE WALL

Climbing in Cuba was like a dream for me. When we arrived in Viñales Valley in 1999, only one route existed. I felt like Layton Kor in the early days of climbing in Eldorado Canyon – the most beautiful, aesthetic lines were just waiting to be climbed. Large pockets, tufas, and stalactites provided access to the radically overhanging walls

I never felt so on fire for climbing. I was obsessed – I had to keep returning to fuel the fire, and to open routes on the biggest, steepest walls we could find. We were constantly amazed that the crazy-steep routes we chose went free, at our far-below-world-class abilities of 5.11 and 5.12. We had to continually devise new strategies for rappelling the overhanging multi-pitch routes so we didn't strand ourselves in space.

I was intrigued with the three-dimensional aspect of the climbing, and the tufas and stalactites that you could pinch, sidepull, hand jam, heel hook, bear hug, or even squeeze between your legs. The hold-generous Cuban limestone provided the most fun style of climbing I had ever done.

But the trips to Cuba were about much more than rock climbing. The beautiful green landscape and red soil gave me a feeling of peace and serenity, and they made it easy to take fantastic landscape photos.

I instantly fell in love with Cuban music – we saw live music almost every night. This mix of Caribbean, African, and Cuban musical styles just make you feel good. When the music started, the Cuban people unconsciously swayed their hips. We were all feeling good.

To my surprise I developed a deep kinship with the unbelievably warm and friendly Cuban people. Initially I expected hostile reactions toward us Americans. After all, the U.S. embargo, coupled with the oppressive Cuban government, made the lives of Cubans very difficult. But every Cuban I interacted with was extremely friendly.

"You live in the United States?" many would ask. "My cousin lives in the United States."

"Really?" I would reply. "In Miami?"

A confused look, followed by, "Yes, how did you know?" was the standard reply.

Most Cubans counter their lack of material wealth with something far more important – a deep love for their family, friends, art, and music. Many of the Cubans seem happier than their counterparts to the north who chase the American dream of a big house, big car, and fat retirement fund.

We immediately bonded with the Cuban climbers, and started the ethic of leaving our gear behind because they had a strong desire to climb, but no way to acquire the equipment.

The Cuban climbers were loaded with talent. Many reached the 5.10 level in just a few days of climbing. It probably helped that they were starving in the early nineties when subsidies from the Soviet empire ceased. It's rare that you see a lick of body fat on a young Cuban.

Vitalio Echazábal became my Cuban brother. We even looked alike after my hair curled up in the thick humidity. When I visited him in Barcelona where he emigrated, it was like no time had passed since we were together. Vitalio has the body of a European rock star – a tiny waist supporting huge lats, biceps, and shoulders – without the years of training.

Aníbal Fernández also showed true talent, and on a visit to the States we climbed *Naked Edge* in Colorado, and *Texas Tower* in southern Utah. Aníbal cruised both routes, though they required hard climbing using techniques he had never seen. I was impressed when he led a decaying chimney on *Texas Tower* with one or two pieces of protection in the entire pitch.

On the Cuba trips I developed deep friendships with a select crew of American partners. I will always have a deep gratitude to Skip Harper for taking me to several Caribbean islands to climb, and for coercing me to accompany him to Cuba; and to Armando Menocal for his assistance with the language and logistics, for arranging our first meeting with the Cuban climbers, and for his incredible work to help the Cuban climbers. Cameron Cross, twenty years my junior, partnered with me to open many routes in Cuba. He remains one of my best friends, and now he has taken over my old role of organizing climbing events in northern Colorado.

I have often said, if I could only keep one set of my climbing adventures over the past three decades, it would be my trips to Cuba. I can't wait for my daughter Giulia to grow older, and the U.S. travel restrictions to ease, so I can return and share with her the magic that I found in this Caribbean paradise.

Craig Luebben - Golden, Colorado, 2009

The Steeps! *Lowering off Pink Lady (6c) with Mr. Mogote Wall as a backdrop.*

CUEVA DE SAN MIGUEL

The wall is easily accessible and, at present, sports only a single route, *Jungle Warfare*. Cueva de San Miguel's isolated setting in a snug valley and potential for multi-pitch routes merits more attention.

APPROACH

The wall is found on the obvious crag at the back of the fields behind the El Palenque disco/restaurant. To reach it, either walk though the tunnel that starts at the bar or hike around on the paved road.

CLIMBING

This wall features an enjoyable multi-pitch climb in a pleasant setting. Check it out!

Cueva de San Miguel

Only one route, so far.

❶ Jungle Warfare 6c ★★★ .. ☐

This climb finishes in a small, but obvious cave with a thread inside it. Pitches 1 and 2 can be linked to prevent rope drag when leading the final crux pitch.

pitch 1 (6b+, 36 M)
pitch 2 (5+, 16 M)
pitch 3 (6c, 8 M)
Descend with two rappels, even with double 60-metre ropes.
3 pitches, bolts FA: *Anna Greissing & Mike Robertson, 2002.*

© YAROBYS GARCÍA

CUBA LIBRE WALL

You won't believe your eyes when you first see this crag! It extends for almost 1 kilometre along the left side of the road by El Palenque bar and nowhere else in Viñales will you find such steep rock "melting" with crazy limestone features. The stalactites and tufas in the caves on Cuba Libre wall are so large they tend to dwarf the average climber, but their great size can be an asset! Even on the steepest routes, sneaky rests can be found by contorting body parts around the alien-like features. The dramatic nature of this cliff caught the eye of early Viñales route developers and Craig Luebben quickly established *Cuba Libre*, the first line on the wall and eventual namesake of the crag.

APPROACH

To access the base of Cuba Libre wall, walk toward the cliff from El Palenque bar and pick up the forested trail behind the left-most buildings. Follow the trail up to the cliff, watching for three different exit points to the various alcoves. Consider landmarking the main cliff features from the meadow besides the parking area before hiking into the forest; it may help in identifying your chosen alcove. This approach takes about 10 minutes from the parking area. Note that Cuba Libre wall is next to El Palenque bar and some administrators are not as climber-friendly as others, so please be respectful.

CLIMBING

For most, it takes some time to get comfortable climbing on such steep, stalactite-riddled terrain, but rest assured the bolts are in solid rock and falls are safe, provided a dynamic belay is provided. Note that a big drop is almost always preferential to a short, swinging fall that may accelerate the climber up into the stalactite daggers! The height and steepness of routes on Cuba Libre wall provide so much exposure that lower-offs into the forest are common. Please be careful with rope lengths and always tie knots in the end of your cords!

The best time to climb here is mid-morning onward, as the only sun penetration is very early in the day. Seepage can be a problem in the rainy season (May–October), but during the prime climbing months the wall should be dry, even in the rain.

Caution: *Please be very careful when belaying at Cuba Libre wall. Tufas can break, especially when a pumped climber is desperately slapping at one!*

Paraíso
Escondido
3RD ALCOVE
2ND ALCOVE
1ST ALCOVE
View from highway

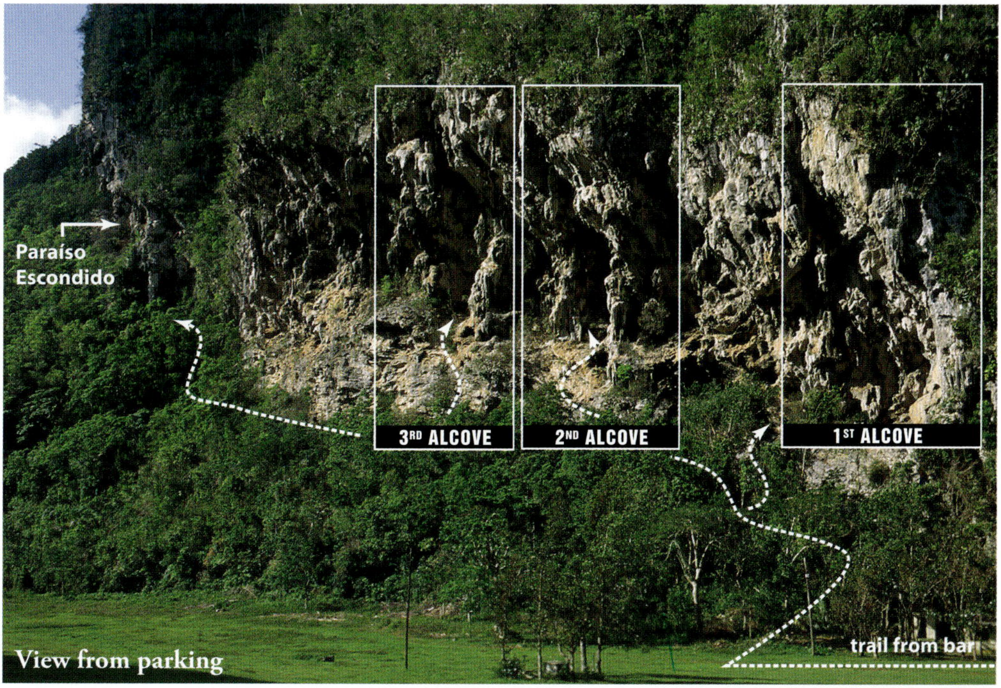

Paraíso
Escondido
3RD ALCOVE
2ND ALCOVE
1ST ALCOVE
View from parking
trail from bar

Moscow Mule (7b) *Sneaking through stalactites on a spectacular pitch of limestone.*

First Alcove

Scramble up the rocks to the right of the main trail and around a boulder until you reach the clear ledge under the right-most overhang.

❶ Nieve de Mayabe 6c ★★★ . . . . ☐

This route climbs the right outside edge of the alcove, starting from the corner at the edge of the ledge. When lowering, have the belayer toss the free end of the rope to the climber to pull back to the ledge. Two ropes will get you all the way down into the trees.

1 pitch (30 M), 10 bolts *FA: Craig Luebben, 1999.*

❷ Najita 6c+ ★★★★★ . . . . ☐

Start on the cracks behind the boulder where you get onto the ledge. The route climbs to

the stalactites and traverses right (crux) to a bolt anchor. It is best to lower from here and avoid rope drag, but if you prefer, two more bolts above connect to *Mayabe*.

1 pitch (30 M), 12 bolts *FA: Craig Luebben & Cameron Cross, 1999.*

Second alcove

Stay on the main trail for a few metres beyond the turnoff to the First Alcove. Watch for an obvious path that leads to the right and up.

❸ Cuba Libre 7a+ ★★★★ . . . . ☐

This excellent route was the first on the wall and is a classic of the grade in Viñales. Some fixed threads supplement the bolts.

pitch 1 (5, 20 M) Start on the first pillar to the right as you enter the alcove. To landmark, look for the fixed threads. Belay under the roof.

pitch 2 (6a+, 20 M) Traverse right and around the corner to a belay under the final roof.

pitch 3 (7a+, 10 M) The upper section is a spectacular roof with a very unusual offwidth move just before the anchors. Bring a second rope for the 50-metre rappel.

3 pitches, bolts *FA: Craig Luebben & George Bracksieck, 1999.*

❹ The Rum Diaries 7b+ ★★★★★ . . . . ☐

This a direct start to *Cuba Libre* and joins that route at the start of the final roof, allowing the wall to be climbed in a single, sustained pitch. The start is reached through a little cave on the right side of this alcove; note that the first bolt is high. The rating and quickdraw count is for the complete route to the rim.

1 pitch (27 M), 13 bolts *FA: Charlie Woodburn, 2002.*

❺ Captain Hook 7b ★★★★★ . . . . ☐

This is a great climb. From inside the Cuba Libre alcove go up left to the highest level.
pitch 1 (7a, 20 M) Start on the first tufas to the right using the fixed thread and climb the steep arête up the right edge of the alcove.
pitch 2 (7b, 10 M) Climb up and left.
2 pitches, bolts *FA: Seb Grieve, 2002.*

❻ Our Man in Havana 7b+ ★★★★ . . . . ☐

This is a slightly harder option to the second pitch of the Captain Hook. Climb rightward from the first anchor.
1 pitch, bolts *FA: Grant Farquhar, 2002.*

❼ Moscow Mule 7b ★★★★ . . . . ☐

Start at the back of the cave and climb the tufas and huecos before moving right. Lots of sneaky rests on this one. Crux at the top!
1 pitch (20 M), **bolts** *FA: Seb Grieve, 2002.*

❽ Pink Lady 6c ★★★ . . . . ☐

This route climbs the column and stalactites on the left side of the alcove. The route is very steep for the grade and wanders through hanging features to finish with a wild stem to a huge, hanging fang. It's very exposed and still a bit dirty. Note that a second climber must follow this route to clean it.
1 pitch (25 M), **bolts** *FA: Mike Robertson, 2002.*

❾ Medico de la Salsa 7a+ ★★★ . . . . . ☐

Start in the next bay, which is reached through the hollow tufa of *Pink Lady*. Follow the bolt-line up and left to join *Pink Lady* near the finish. Since the full route is 60 metres, you need two ropes to rappel and a partner to toprope the route to clean the quickdraws.
1 pitch (60 M), **bolts** *FA: Grant Farqhuar & Anna Greissing, 2002.*

Third Alcove

The lower trail leads into the final alcove.

❿ Pollo del Mar 7a ★★★★ . . . . ☐

Start on top of the tufa pillar on the right of the alcove and follow the bolts rightward along the ramp. Finish on a big, hanging stalactite. This climb is very exposed and a bit runout, but the falls are clean. Use a double-rope rappel to descend.
1 pitch (50 M), **bolts** *FA: Grant Farqhuar & Mike Robertson, 2002.*

⓫ One Percent 6c+ ★★★★ . . . . ☐

This route starts in the back of the alcove and weaves up and out to dangling stalactites. Long slings might help with potential rope-drag issues!
1 pitch (30 M), **10 bolts** *FA: Cameron Cross, 2000.*

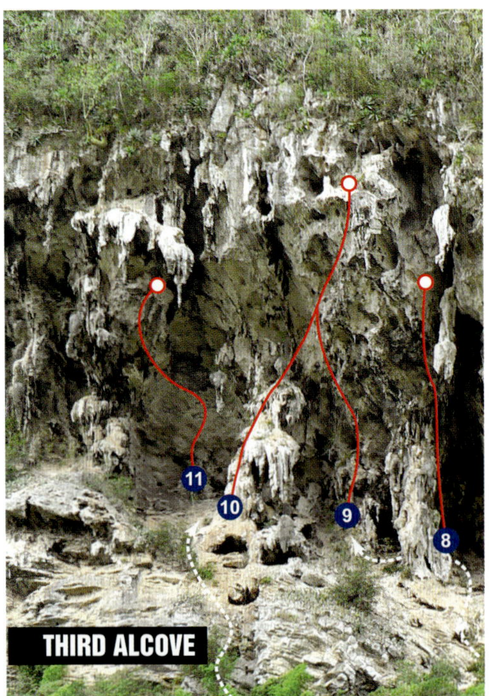

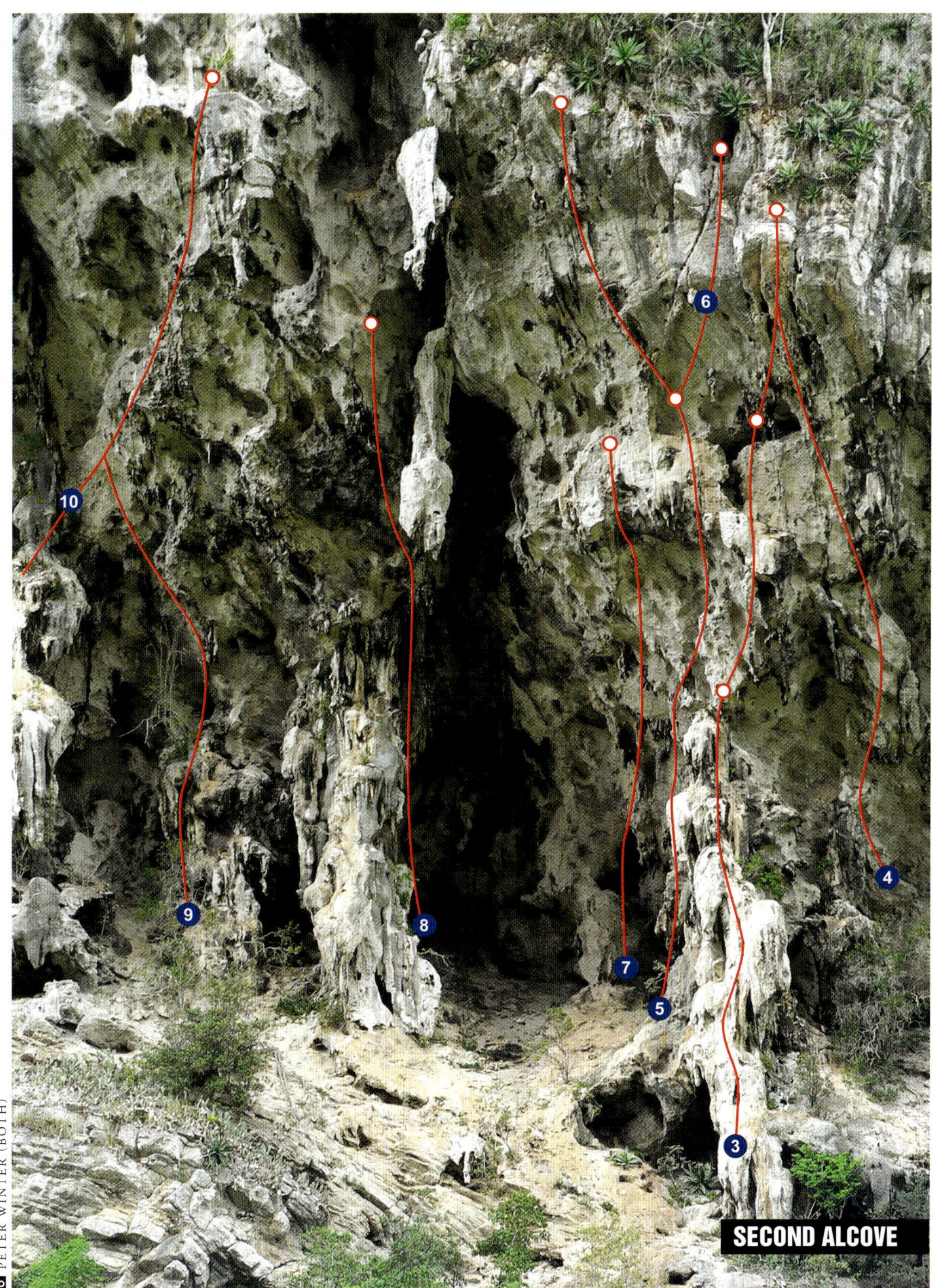
SECOND ALCOVE

PARAÍSO ESCONDIDO

Paraíso Escondido – Secluded Paradise – is the next big cavern of alcoves and tufa columns left of Cuba Libre wall and includes the obvious, white free-standing column of *Colmillo Blanco*. This amazing crag has seen little development since the first route was established in 2000. This is probably due to the cliff's distance from Viñales and the lack of mechanized transportation available to most locals. However, for visiting climbers, Paraíso Escondido is well-sheltered from the elements and the overhang provides plenty of stalactites and hanging chandeliers to keep you busy for a day.

APPROACH

The direct trail starts at the edge of the field below the crag, but it's tough to follow as it's frequently being reclaimed by the jungle. If you persist, however, and keep wandering upwards you will soon come to *Colmillo Blanco*. Alternatively, approach along the trail that accesses Cuba Libre wall. Avoid entering any of the three alcoves by continuing along the lower (main) trail. Eventually, the trail will drop down before ascending to the base of *Colmillo Blanco*. To reach the higher alcove at Paraíso Escondido, climb the first pitch of *Colmillo Blanco* and then traverse left and through a small cave, which puts you at the base of the climbs. Alternatively, from *Colmillo Blanco*, drop down and hike leftward around the lower cliff-band to access the alcove with the routes. Total approach time is about 15 minutes from the parking area.

THE CLIMBING

This alcove is slightly beyond and above the Cuba Libre wall and every bit as bizarre and impressive. One of the early routes through the unique labyrinth of limestone features had the working name *Dagas del Cielo* (Hanging Daggers), an apt description of rock, but that name didn't stick. This wall features acrobatic climbing on steep ground with a very exotic feel.

Comillo Blanco

PARAÍSO ESCONDIDO
CUBA LIBRE WALL
View from highway

PARAÍSO ESCONDIDO
El palenque
CUBA LIBRE WALL

Paraíso Escondido

The classic line here – Psicodriller – is a four-pitch route that crosses overhangs, moves around huge stalactites and reaches a wild suspended cavern. Routes are listed from left to right.

❶ Psico Driller 6c ★★★★★ . . . . ☐

If you want to climb a long steep line at a moderate level, this is your route. Every pitch is overhanging and the third pitch climbs a roof full of features. Bring two ropes and some long slings.

pitch 1 (6b, 25 M) Start in a crack up the initial overhang. Straight up to the belay.

pitch 2 (6c, 30 M) Exit the anchor moving down and left. Arch left to an anchor in a cave under the stalactite-studded roof.

pitch 3 (6c+, 25 M) Look for the bolts on the other side of the column, to the left of the belay. Climb out the roof to a short, steep section and finish on a ledge with the anchor.

pitch 4 (6a, 30 M) Take the obvious line and finish in a small cave. Rappel 30 metres to the previous anchor and then 60 metres to the ground. Fun!

4 pitches, bolts *FA: Aníbal Fernández & David Ryan, 2002.*

❷ Santanilla 6c+ ★★★ . . . . ☐

This is an alternate start to *Psicodriller*. It climbs the stalactite to the right instead of the original crack.

1 pitch (15 M), bolts *FA: Josué Millo.*

❸ Venciendo el Miedo 6c ★★★ . . . . ☐

The most recent addition to the wall tackles a chimney on the right side of the alcove next to the initial pitches of *Psicodriller*. Do a double-rope rappel to descend.

2 pitches, bolts *FA: Jorge Luís & Yarobys García, 2007.*

❹ Colmillo Blanco 6a ★★★★ . . . . ☐

This is the original route that ascends the big, white free-standing column.

pitch 1 (5+, 20 M) Start on the inside and circle around clock-wise, using threads and big cams for protection. Finish out a small, 2-bolt roof.

pitch 2 (6a, 15 M) Walk to the back of the

wall for a short, overhanging section. This pitch is fully bolted.

2 pitches, mixed *FA: Craig Luebben & David Ryan, 2000.*

⑤ T.P.R. 5+ ★★★★★ . . . . □

This route climbs directly up the valley side of the *Colmillo Blanco* column and avoids the gear necessary for the original start. This is a recommended variation for those without a rack of cams. The name is a reference to a Cuban tooth remedy.

1 pitch (20 M), bolts *FA: David Ryan, 2000.*

CHAPTER 5

MOGOTE DE LOS HOYOS

This impressive wall is located 11 kilometres northeast of Viñales and is a great example of western Cuba's barely-explored "big-wall" sport climbing potential. The 150-metre high by 400-metre wide central wall is hung with imposing caverns, massive tufas and hanging stalactites that resemble gargoyles when seen from afar.

In 2001, Aníbal Fernández and Craig Luebben climbed the first line on the face and, since then, the wall has not garnered another route. It *feels* remote: there are no other routes or climbers and it is far from the towns and villages. Additionally, the views across the hundred-square miles of rolling, verdant farmlands and forests are staggering and add to the sense of isolation. For locals, this wall is hard to access due to the lack of public transportation and hitch-hiking possibilities; however, the potential for multi-pitch sport climbing here is huge and the ambience is one of adventure!

MOGOTE DE LOS HOYOS

APPROACH

Drive north out of Viñales – a taxi to the cliff should cost about $5 CUC, each way. After about four kilometres, turn right onto the paved road that goes to República de Chile and La Palma (see area map on cover). This road may not be signed, but it's the only paved turnoff on the right, just before reaching El Palenque. Once on the correct road, drive past a right turnoff into República de Chile (a "modern" *comunidad* of high-rises) and then take the next right at about 11 kilometres. This accesses the front of the towering wall of Mogote de los Hoyos, which should have been visible from the road long before. Park close to the houses on the roadside and try to landmark the route from below by looking for a lone Drago Palm that grows near the end of the first pitch. The trail starts in the trees directly in front of the cliff and reaches the base of the wall on its right side.

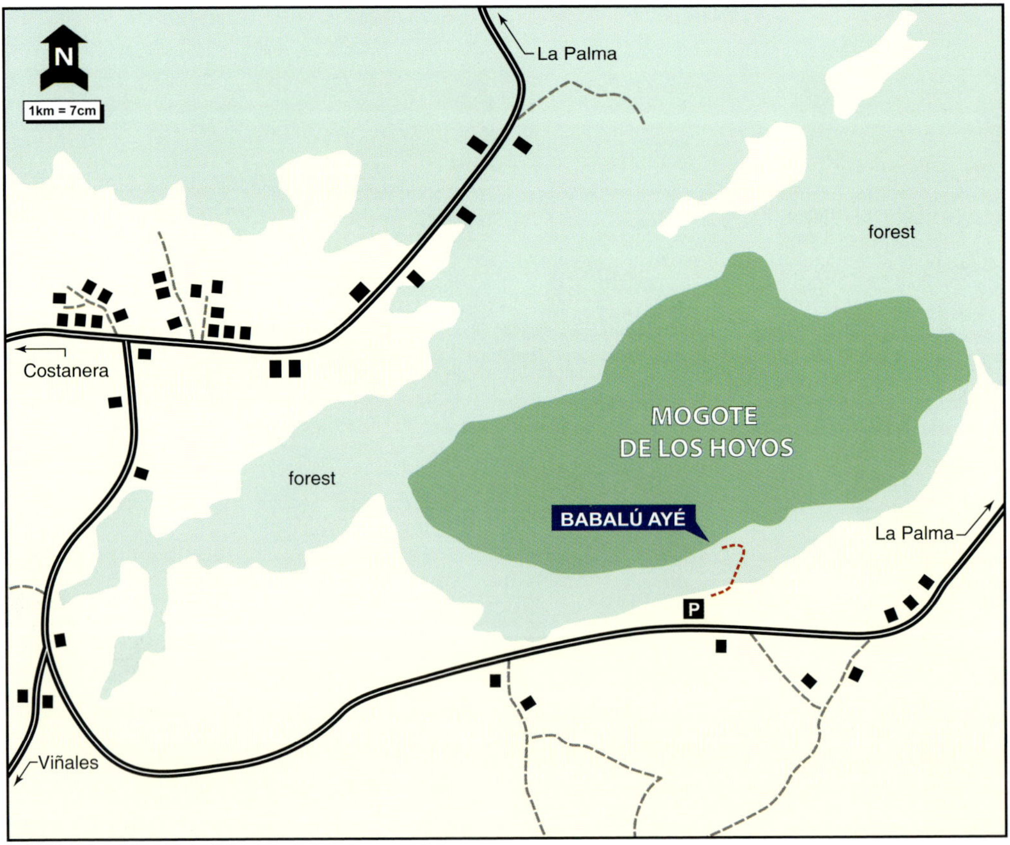

Follow the base left to a grey wall where the ground is clear of vegetation. Look for bolts amidst the delicate looking lattices and honeycombs. These features are much more solid than they look. The approach is about 15 minutes uphill from the parking area.

Alternate approach: Ride a mountain bike on the primitive dirt road that stretches from above the La Ermita Hotel to República de Chile. This ride follows a visually stunning ridge, is consistent with the adventurous nature of the day and is a shorter approach!

THE CLIMBING

Babalú Ayé is a template against which all Cuba climbs should be judged and is definitely worth the extra effort of getting there. It's a fully-bolted adventure, with steep moves and a challenging descent in the middle of a stunning setting. Bring two ropes, lots of water and webbing to replace sun-baked anchors. This wall is in the midday sun most of the year; it's best to wait for a cloudy or cool day to maximize your enjoyment!

Mogote de los Hoyos *Looking up at the wall and the singular climbing objective from the parking area at the road below the crag.*

Mogote de los Hoyos

Currently, there is only one route on this impressive cliff.

❶ Babalú Ayé 6b+ ★★★★★ . . . . ☐

This route follows a line up the centre of the wall, climbing mostly on overhanging terrain, but with belays on comfortable ledges. Bring 13 quickdraws, two 60-metre ropes for the descent and a selection of slings and carabiners to guide the rope around features.

pitch 1 (6a+, 35 M) Start on the narrow grey tufa using some delicate holds and finish with good jugs. The belay is on a ledge up a ramp to the left.

pitch 2 (6b, 33 M) Climb up the low angle section to the right. The first bolt is not visible from the anchors. Once you reach the stalactites, traverse right to climb the pitch's crux and finish with some easy climbing on broken terrain. Belay from inside the alcove/ledge, *not* from the rappel anchors below.

pitch 3 (6b+, 37 M) Exit the ledge on the right and climb big tufas. Move around the corner to a short crux with lots of exposure. Climb a few more metres to a good ledge, then around a slight corner to the left. Clip a thread and then continue up. A few more bolts lead to the belay ledge, home to some vultures.

pitch 4 (6b, 30 M) The last pitch climbs the remaining overhang and starts to the right. It is best to lower back to the ledge because the pitch is short, diagonal and ends in a hanging belay.

Descent: Lower off the top pitch as mentioned above. For the next rappel, it is best to leave the second rope secured to the anchor below during the ascent. This provides a mandatory hand line for pulling into the belay ledge. From here a double, free-hanging rappel will put you on the ledge at the top of pitch 1. Walk up the slope to get to the anchors and pull your partner in as they rappel. From here another 30-metre rappel reaches the ground.

Caution: Extreme care should be taken with the rappels on this route. Ensure the rope pulls smoothly *before* the last person leaves the anchors. Also, place knots at the end of the ropes and always use a prussik back-up. There is a real risk of being stranded in space with no one to help if you blow it.

4 pitches, bolts FA: *Aníbal Fernández & Craig Luebben, 2001.*

Babalú Ayé (6b+) *Aníbal Fernández is dwarfed by the tufas on pitch 3.*

lower
rap with anchored rope
free-hanging rap
rap
1
MOGOTE DE LOS HOYOS

CHAPTER 6

LA COSTANERA

La Costanera is a large, north-facing wall unlike anything else around Viñales. The central sector – La Bóveda de las Españolas – is a very unique cathedral-shaped alcove and perhaps the most majestic wall in all of Cuba. It has great ambience, providing views of the Gulf of Mexico from the higher pitches and it stays in the shade all day, year-round.

This cliff is home to 30-plus pitches of great, multi-pitch sport climbing with potential for many more and contains some of Cuba's signature routes. It's also quite likely that this cliff was the scene of the very first technical rock climb in all of Cuba. Early evidence, in the form of rusted pitons, has been discovered on the wall; the pitons remain in-situ beside a modern anchor. This likely marks the high-point reached by the mysterious team.

LA COSTANERA APPROACH

La Costanera is the original name of the area, but local non-climbers also know it as "Planta de Asfalto", referring to the asphalt plant that once existed near the base. Being familiar with both names might be useful if asking for directions.

This area is technically not part of the Viñales valley or the national park. It is located on the north side of a different range known as the Sierra de San Vicente, 11.5 kilometres north of the town of Viñales. A taxi ride will cost about $5 CUC each way and you can arrange a pick-up time for when you finish climbing. Hitchhiking is feasible, but it gets harder to catch a ride back to town at the end of the day. The few trucks and tractors that go by will likely be full.

To get to La Costanera, take the road that heads north out of Viñales to the *entronque* (split) to Puerto Esperanza and La Palma. Go left toward Puerto Esperanza and promptly start watching for the obvious walls on the left side of the road. There is a big open area for parking by the forest below the wall.

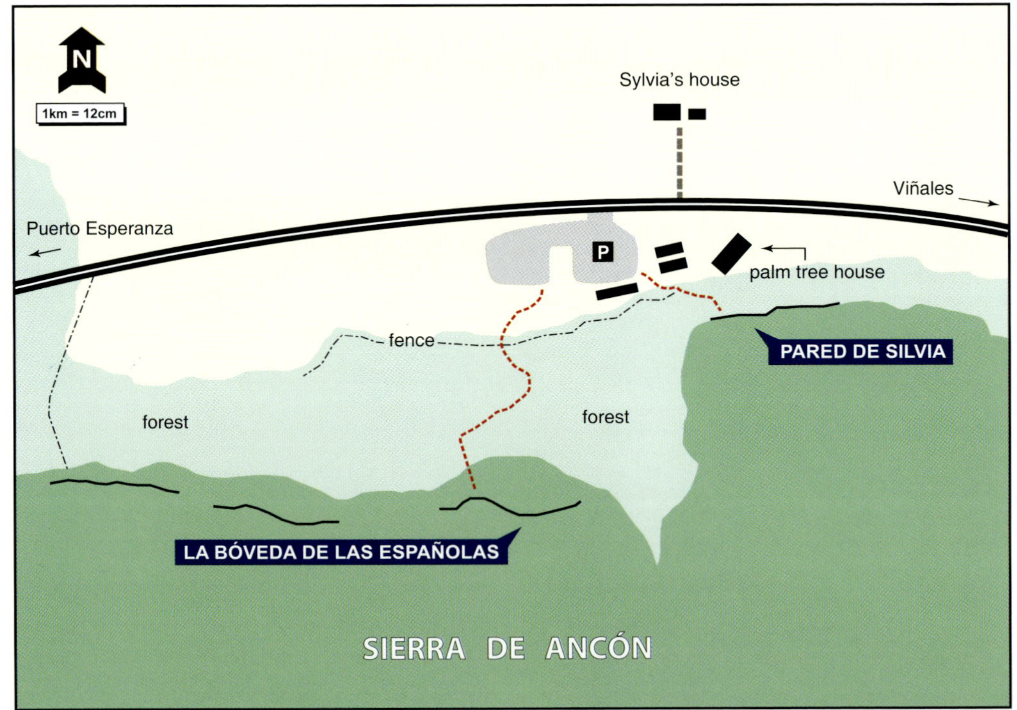

Flyin' Hyena (7b) *This climb was the first route on the main wall and remains a classic "must do" for able visitors. In this picture, Naomi Guy tackles the diagonal crack traverse on pitch 3, which is rated 6c.*

The Palm Tree House *This odd structure is a government facility or "party house" that sits below Pared de Silvia. It's not open to the public and is vacant most of the time.*

Have a Cigar *The sideways scoops on this pitch force climbers to perform some of the strangest moves encountered on rock. Here, Neil Gresham of the UK guns for the 8a redpoint. Most climbers interested in the upper pitches of* Have a Cigar (6c+) *utilize an alternative and much easier start on another route.*

LA BÓVEDA DE LAS ESPAÑOLAS

This is, by far, the most impressive wall in all of Cuba and the routes are all jewels, deserving of the highest star ratings. Craig Luebben discovered this cliff while exploring around Viñales and was so impressed that he came back to climb the very first lines shortly thereafter. Lucky him!

APPROACH

After you park, look for the start of the trail behind a fence and below the main wall. The trail wanders uphill through the forest and reaches the crag on its right side in about five minutes. Follow the wall to the right for the first three routes and go left for everything else, including the *Have a Cigar* cave, which is a good place to drop your gear and take shelter from the weather.

THE CLIMBING

The "cathedral" contains magnificent rock, exposed pitches, technical rappels, a variety of grades and guaranteed satisfaction! It's so steep that the top pitches of the multi-pitch climbs (as well as the routes in the big cave) stay dry in the rain. Bring two 60-metre ropes, a few slings or carabiners to back-up rappel anchors and please follow the specific route descent instructions to avoid ending up stranded in the space without a way to get back to the wall!

Note: Signs of corrosion have been found on some of the bolts on this wall. This is likely due to the proximity of the cliff to the sea, so some rebolting has been done. Check with locals for the latest information, although in general, every climb is very well-bolted.

La Bóveda de las Españolas

Mucho Pumpito (6b) *In the midst of rock climbing paradise!*

Approach Trail Right

The first routes are to the right of where the trail meets the cliff and are listed from left to right. They are not shown on the photograph.

❶ Centro de Referencia 7a ★★★★ ... ☐

This climb starts about 30 metres from the point at which the main trail hits the wall.
1 pitch (27 M), bolts *FA: Josué Millo & Jusnier Blanco, 2005.*

❷ Problemas de Conexion 7a ★★★★ ☐

This is the next line to the right.
1 pitch (30 M), bolts *FA: Josué Millo & Fransua Bosmenier, 2004.*

❸ Project .... ☐

The bolting may be incomplete on this open project, the last line on the wall.
1 pitch (30 M), bolts? *Prep: Josué Millo & Jusnier Blanco, 2005.*

Central Wall

The remaining routes are all left of the point where the approach trail meets the wall.

❹ Nueva Vida 6c ★★★★ .... ☐

Upon reaching the wall, this is the first route left of the approach trail. Start on the pocketed orange face above the easy ramp. The crux is below the chain anchors.
1 pitch (27 M), bolts *FA: Javier Alvarez & Vitalio Echazábal, 1999.*

❺ Viernes Trece 7a ★★★★★ .... ☐

This route is a three-pitch continuation of *Nueva Vida* up the right side of the big arête.
pitch 1: *Nueva Vida* (6c, 27 M)
pitch 2: (5, 25 M) Easy climbing leads to a belay in a little cave.
pitch 3 (6a+, 25 M) Climb left and up, mantle the flake and enjoy! And finish the pitch.

pitch 4 (7a, 24 M) Follow the leaning hand crack left of the anchors to some steep tufas. The exit to the top anchors could be dirty.
Descent: You must leave a 60-metre tag-line tied to the second belay anchor in order to pull yourself back into the wall as you rappel from the top of pitch 4. A second 60-metre rappel will put you on the ground.
4 pitches, bolts *FA: Vitalio Eschazabal, 2001.*

❻ El Lamento de los Toros 7a ★★★★ ☐

This climb starts right of the corner and ascends to the chain anchors of *Visado Familiar*.
1 pitch (30 M), bolts *FA: Martín Moline & Ariel Pasqueletti.*

❼ Visado Familiar 6c ★★★★ .... ☐

Start left of the visible corner on a light grey arête, five metres to the right of the root that marks the start of *Flyin' Hyena*. The chains are the best lowering option if you only want to climb this pitch, otherwise belay from the ledge on the left to continue up *Chicken Run*.
1 pitch (30 M), bolts *FA: José Naranjo, 1999.*

❽ Chicken Run 7a+ ★★★★★ .... ☐

This route is the three-pitch continuation of *Visado Familiar* and follows the eye-catching dihedral on the right side of the Costanera "cathedral". It's possible to descend this route with one 60-metre rope, but two ropes are recommended.
pitch 1 *Visado Familiar* (6c, 30 M)
pitch 2 (6c, 30 M) Beware of loose rock as you exit the belay ledge and then climb a slab before getting into the dihedral. Sustained moves will bring you to a small ledge.
pitch 3 (7a, 25 M) Start in the dihedral and then move left to climb pockets and huecos around the bushes. Re-enter the corner and stem upwards to the belay cave. Use caution with the boulder on the ledge.
pitch 4 (7a+, 25 M) Ascend the wide crack

above the ledge, execute a cruxy face move and then traverse the roof right to finish.
Descent (1 rope): After leading the fourth pitch, extend the anchor with slings to prevent rope-drag and then get lowered back to the anchors on the third pitch. The second will need to toss a rope-end to the leader to help pull back into the anchor. The second then cleans pitch 4 and gets lowered back down to the anchor on top of pitch 3. Pull the rope and then rappel to *Flyin' Hyena's* second belay. Two 30-metre rappels reach the ground.
Descent (2 ropes): Leave a 60-metre tag-line tied to the second belay anchor. Rappel 60 metres from the top to the pitch 2 anchor and then another 60 metres to the ground.
4 pitches, bolts *FA: Aníbal Fernández & David Ryan, 2001.*

❾ ¡Viva la Libertad! 7b ★★★★ . . . . ☐

This variation links *Visado Familiar* with the top pitches of *Viernes Thirteen*. From the ledge anchor atop *Visado Familiar*, climb the face and the tufas to the right of the big dihedral. If climbing to the top, leave a tag line clipped to the top anchor and rappel the route.
1 pitch, bolts *FA: Lynn Hill, 2006.*

❿ Flyin' Hyena 7b ★★★★★ . . . . ☐

This is the big, classic multi-pitch climb of the Costanera "cathedral" and was the first route on the wall. It has a stunning setting, mysterious history, big-wall exposure and acrobatic climbing. The original first pitch started by climbing a large tree root. A hurricane killed the tree and now the root is unsafe. Some bolts have been added for an alternate start, but the first eight metres remain unprotected. Bring two 60-metre ropes.

pitch 1 (6, 30 M, 6 bolts) Climb to the left of the root (soloing, essentially) until you reach the first bolt on a small ledge. Follow cracks leftward to a little cave with a thread and then continue to the bolted belay station on the ledge above. The old pitons, perlon and carabiner are from an early, unrecorded attempt to climb the wall and should not be removed; they are part of Cuban climbing history.

pitch 2 (6a+, 25 M, 6 bolts) Traverse right and climb the far side of the tufa. Belay on the top.

pitch 3 (6c, 25 M, 7 bolts) The diagonal crack will bring you to the tufas on the left. Belay on a ledge above.

pitch 4 (7a, 25 M, 7 bolts) Move up and right from the anchors. Climb a bouldery face section before reaching the tufas that bring you to the base of the roof.

pitch 5 (7b, 15 M, 8 bolts) Climb the left side of the roof and enjoy the exposure! Note that pitch 4 and 5 can be linked at 7b+ with 15 quickdraws and some long slings to reduce rope-drag. This avoids the hanging belay.

Descent: Leave a tag-line clipped to the third belay station to pull back in from the top of pitch 5. From here, a 60-metre rappel leads to the anchor on the first pitch. One more rappel leads to the ground.
5 pitches, bolts *FA: Craig Luebben, Cameron Cross & Armando Menocal, 2000.*

⓫ Ruta de los Italianos 8a+? ★★★ . . . ☐

This route crisscrosses the wall, climbing improbable faces and linking a couple of the original routes. It's hard, a bit contrived and the ratings are uncertain. No repeat ascents are known. Finish up the last pitch of *Flyin' Hyena* and descend as for that route.
4 pitches, bolts *FA: Gianni Faggianna & Massimo Iacolare.*

⓬ La Preferida 6b ★★★★ . . . . ☐

A dead tree right of the cave and two closely-spaced bolts very near the ground mark the start of this route. Climb bouldery moves to a ramp. Follow cracks and huecos to a cave.
1 pitch, bolts *FA: Rosanno Boscarino, 2000.*

⓭ Mercenario 7c ★★★★★ . . . . ☐

This is a three-pitch continuation up the wall above *La Preferida*. Aníbal Fernández improved *La Preferida* (now popular) and then established the upper pitches – *Mercenario* – each with a different partner. The last pitch was established solo because Fernández couldn't find a belayer!

pitch 1: *La Preferida* (6b)

pitch 2 (6b+) Follow the steep crack system to the next alcove.

pitch 3 (7c) Stem up the big tufas and follow the bolts to the right. A series of powerful moves will take you out the roof. Once you hit the blank face above, traverse right to the anchors on top of the huge stalactite. A strong climber should follow this pitch since it is virtually impossible to lower back to the belay. To avoid this pitch, see *Variante Compota*.

pitch 4 (6a) Easy climbing leads to the top of the wall.

Descent: Bring two 60-metre ropes. Rappel or lower 30 metres from the pitch 4 anchor to the top of pitch 3. From here, a 60-metre rappel will *barely* reach the ground. Enjoy the exposure!

4 pitches, bolts *FA: Aníbal Fernández, Josué Millo & Gianni Faggiana, 2003.*

⓮ Variante Compota 6c ★★★★ . . . . . ☐

This is an easier variation for the third pitch of *Mercenario* and links that route with *Have a Cigar*. Once you exit the second belay, climb left instead of right. Steep tufas lead to a wicked stem section. This pitch joins *Have a Cigar* around the corner. Descend as for *Have a Cigar*.

Link-up: The combination of *Mercenario*, *Compota* and *Have a Cigar* is the easiest path to the top of the wall, climbing to its highest point at only 6c. This is a highly recommended variation.

1 pitch, bolts *FA: Aníbal Fernández, 2002.*

© YAROBYS GARCÍA

13
10
14
10
11
10
11
17
13
8
9
5
16
15
12
10
7
6
4

⑮ Pablo's Squirmfest 6a ★★★★★ ...☐

This fun, moderate route accesses the top pitches of *Have a Cigar* for mere mortals and is also a popular warm-up for the other climbs in the area. Start on the right edge of the cavern, at the base of some column-like tufas and climb steep jugs to an alcove. Two additional bolts and a technical move after the anchor link this route with the second pitch of *Have a Cigar*.

1 pitch (15 M), 7 bolts *FA: David Ryan, 2000.*

⑯ Have a Cigar (p1) 8a ★★★★★ .....☐

The original first pitch of *Have a Cigar* has some of the funkiest moves you will ever do. It starts inside the main cave and the first ascentionist used a charred tree limb as aid to reach the initial holds on the stalactite. The climb then goes sideways through bizarre scoops and is awkwardly technical (7c Ao). To bypass the Ao opening, Neil Gresham added a few bolts for a "sit-down" start from the back wall (8a).

1 pitch (25 M), bolts *FA: Craig Luebben & Cameron Cross, 2000. FA (cave start): Neil Gresham, 2002.*

⑰ Have a Cigar 7a ★★★★★ ....☐

Since following the original first pitch of *Have a Cigar* is practically impossible and unclipping can lead to a ground-fall, we recommend starting on *Pablo's Squirmfest*. It's more consistent with the nature of the wall and much safer.

pitch 1 *Pablo's Squirmfest* (6a, 15 M)
pitch 2 (6c, 30 M) Surmount the first little roof and climb the crack to a crux at its top. Follow bolts between the big tufas to a small ledge belay.
pitch 3 (7A, 30 M) Climb the gorgeous tufa rib to a hanging belay.
pitch 4 (6b, 25 M) The hardest moves are leaving the anchors at the start of the pitch.
Descent: Bring two 60-metre ropes. Rap with one rope from the top to the pitch 3 anchor. From here, make a 60-metre rappel to the ground.

4 pitches, bolts *FA (above Pablo's Squirmfest): Craig Luebben & Cameron Cross, 2000.*

⑱ Pssst! 7a+ ★★★★★ ....☐

This is the first route on the left side of the main cave. Follow the path on the left of the alcove and turn right and up to a sloping ledge. Watch your steps!

pitch 1 (6b+) The first bolts are in the groove above your head as you exit the cave. Climb this groove, traverse right (runout) and back left to finish on *Mucho Pumpito's* anchors.
pitch 2 (6a) Climb the second pitch of *Mucho Pumpito*.
pitch 3 (7a+) Climb up and left off the ledge. Descend by lowering from the pitch 3 anchor to the belay atop pitch 2. Make a 60-metre free-hanging rappel from here to the ground.

3 pitches, bolts *FA: Craig Luebben & Cameron Cross, 2000.*

⑲ Mucho Pumpito 6b (7a+) ★★★★★ ☐

If there is a single **must-do** route in Viñales, this has *got* to be it. The second pitch is one of the steepest and most enjoyable 6b routes you will likely ever climb and it's easy to rappel off without doing the final 7a+ pitch. It's interesting to note that *Mucho Pumpito* is actually a link-up of the first pitch of an old David Ryan route and the second pitch of *Pssst*, a multi-pitch route climbed by Cameron Cross and Craig Luebben. Since each route was originally a complete climb to the rim, there are two options for a third pitch, but neither is actually part of *Mucho Pumpito*. Bring two 60-metre ropes to descend and a few long slings for use as threads on the 6b pitch.

pitch 1 (6a+, 25 M, 6 bolts) Follow the approach indicated for the previous route. The first pitch starts on the free-standing column and climbs in and out of a little cave. Keep the belayer tied to the column until you clip the first bolt and use a long sling to clip the bolt inside the cave. Follow delicate looking flakes to the belay ledge.

pitch 2 (6b, 30 M, 10 bolts) This is it – possibly the best 6b you will *ever* do! Climb the overhanging arête on jugs so big they are better described as handlebars. This pitch is very steep and exposed, but has an incredible no-hands rest on the stalactite midway up. Savour the moment. Rappel or …

pitch 3 (7a+, 15/25 M, bolts) There are two options for a third pitch, both 7a+. The short and bouldery left option is the original third pitch of *Pssst*. The right option is longer and is David Ryan's original pitch 3.

Descent: If you do a third pitch, lower back to the belay station on the top of pitch 2. Make an awesome 60-metre free-hanging rappel from here to the ground.

3 pitches, bolts *FA: Craig Luebben, Cameron Cross & David Ryan, 2000.*

⑳ Wish You Were Here 7a ★★★ . . . . . ☐

Start in the groove left of *Mucho Pumpito*.
pitch 1 (7a, 25 M, 8 bolts) Climb an overhanging crack to the *Mucho Pumpito* belay.
pitch 2 (6b+, 35 M, 8 bolts) Clip the first two bolts of *Mucho Pumpito* and then move left, protecting in the cracks using nuts, Tricams and medium camming units. Finish the pitch by climbing the bolted overhang.
Descent: Bring two 60-metre ropes to rappel.
2 pitches, mixed *FA: Craig Luebben & Cameron Cross, 2000.*

Mucho Pumpito Ledge

The next three routes start on the big ledge left of Mucho Pumpito's first station. Climb Mucho's first pitch to access the ledge or scramble around to the left. Beware of the cave-like hole on the ledge that goes all the way to the ground!

© ANDREW BURR

㉑ Mucho Mosquito 7a+ ★★★★ . . . . . ☐

This fine pitch climbs the tufas to the left of *Wish You Were Here*. To descend, lower back to the ledge and then rappel 30 metres to the ground from *Mucho Pumpito's* first belay anchor.
1 pitch (30 M), 16 bolts *FA: Brad Lynch & Ned Harris.*

㉒ Sosa Cáustica 7a ★★★★ . . . . ☐

Climb cracks above the ledge "hole". Finish on *Mucho Mosquito*; use the same descent.
1 pitch (30 M), bolts *FA: Aníbal Fernández & Josué Millo, 2003.*

㉓ Diedro de Oshún 7a+ ★★★★ . . . . . ☐

Go to the left edge of the ledge and belay from big threads. Start climbing up the obvious column and continue in the golden dihedral above. Use the same descent as before.
1 pitch (30 M), bolts *FA: Aníbal Fernández, 2003.*

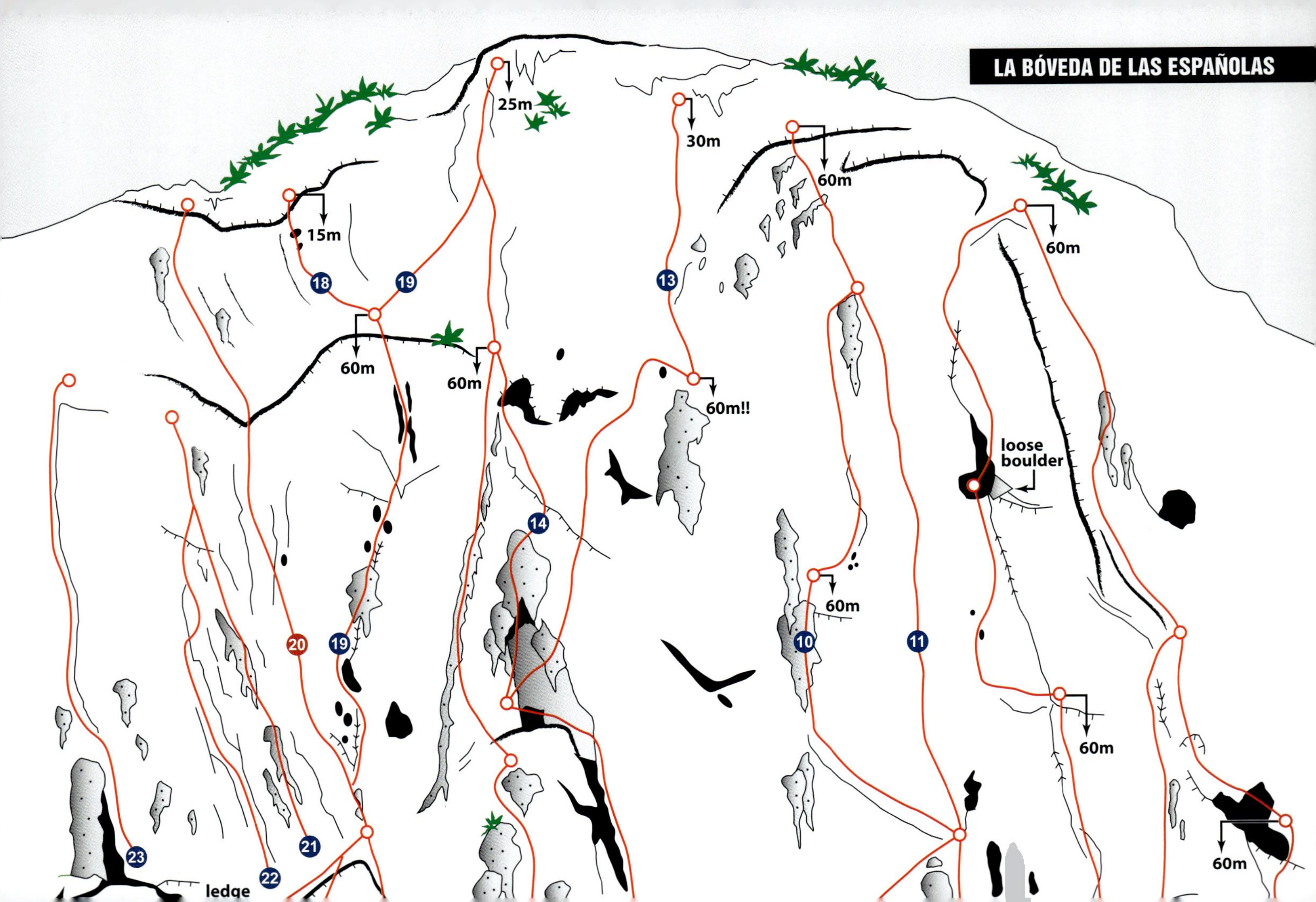

LA BÓVEDA DE LAS ESPAÑOLAS
25m
30m
60m
15m
18
19
13
60m
60m
60m!!
60m
14
loose boulder
10
11
20
19
60m
60m
23
21
22
ledge
60m

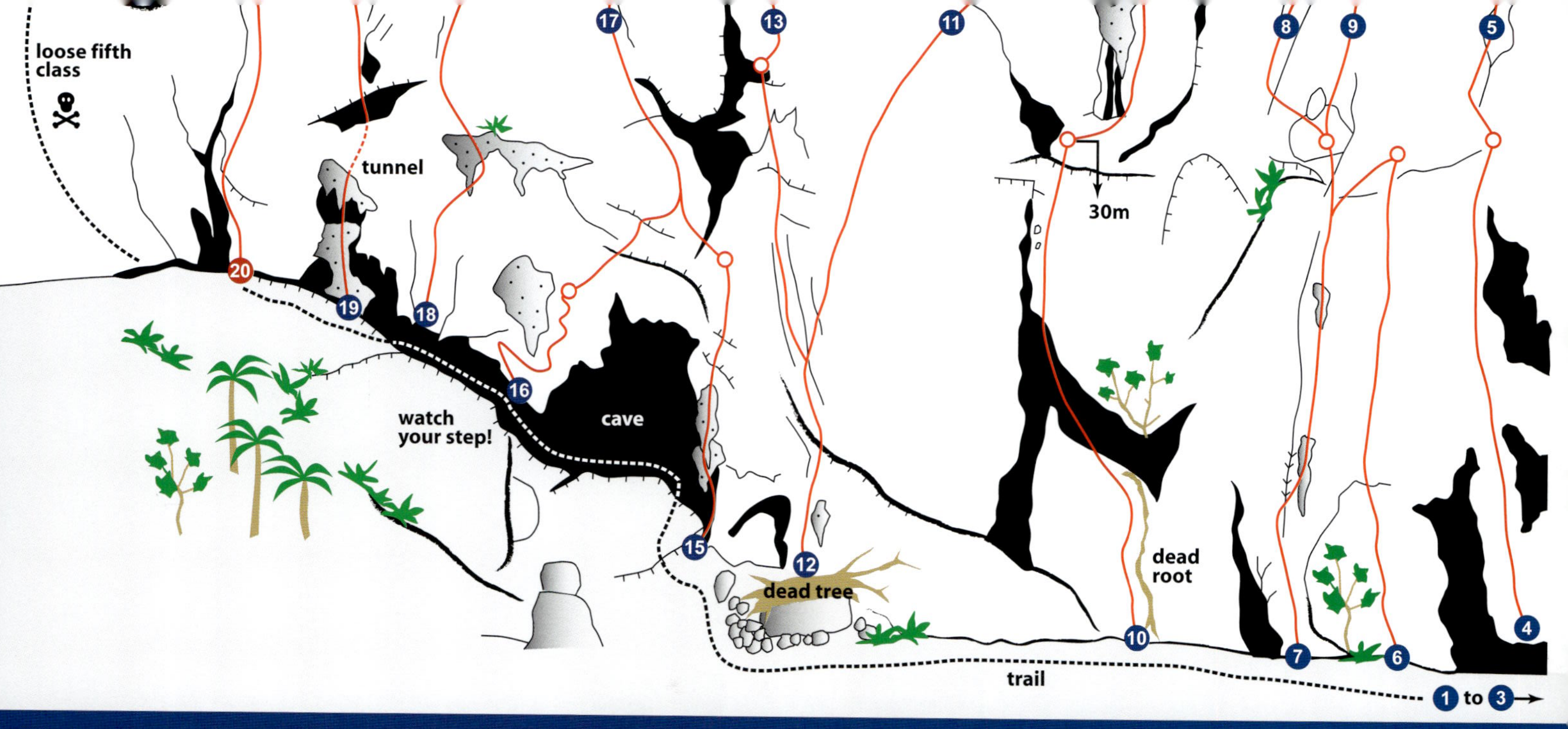

loose fifth class
tunnel
30m
watch your step!
cave
dead tree
dead root
trail
1 to 3
1 Centro de Referencia (7a)
2 Problemas de Conexion (7a)
3 Project
4 Nueva Vida (6c)
5 Viernes Thirteen (7a)
6 El Lamento de los Toros (7a)
7 Visado Familiar (6c)
8 Chicken Run (7a+)
9 ¡Viva la Libertad! (7b)
10 Flyin' Hyena (7b)
11 Ruta de los Italianos (8a+)
12 La Preferida (6b)
13 Mercenario (7c)
14 Variante Compota (6c)
15 Pablo's Squirmfest (6a)
16 Have a Cigar P1 (8a)
17 Have a Cigar (7a)
18 Pssst! (7a+)
19 Mucho Pumpito (6b/7a+)
20 Wish You Were Here (7a)
21 Mucho Mosquito (7a+)
22 Sosa Cáustica (7a)
23 Diedro de Oshún (7a+)

Necessity is the mother of invention, and this I saw first-hand on my Caribbean journey. The people and towns of Cuba have been locked in a time capsule for almost 50 years, in what they call *el bloqueo* (the blockade). Amidst the ornate but crumbling facades, tangled overhead wires and diesel-belching antique cars, exists a deep-seated sense of ingenuity driven not only by a lack of raw materials, but also by an abundance of optimism and a tremendous zest for life. Apothecaries stocked with locally-grown herbal remedies, quirky ad hoc storefronts hawking homemade pizza, and bicycle inner tubes repaired so many times that the patches get patched, vividly illustrate not only the need to succeed, but also that wonderful maxim, where there's a will there's a way. In Pinar del Río, the province of tobacco and the epicentre of steep limestone, the wide range of quality sport climbs exemplifies that resourcefulness – routes needed opening so Cuba birthed a climbing scene.

Like most climbers, I thrive on a diverse and active lifestyle, and since childhood I've loved to run, kick, hit and catch. On the Cuban streets and playing fields, my keen eyes were often met by curios gazes from locals, typically followed by enthusiastic invitations to join whatever game was currently in motion. Encouraging shouts of "*venga yuma*" would bounce across the fields. Whether it was an improvised game of baseball (Cuba's national obsession) played with a plastic soda-bottle cap pitched to a knobby, whittled tree branch, or fleet footed *niños* hustling over cobbled stones in frenzied pursuit of a ricocheting ball crafted out of crushed cardboard and tape, it was game on. Any occasion to elevate the heart rate and hone foot, hip and arm synchronization is popular and epitomizes the Cuban "joie de vivre". An early appreciation for physical fitness mixed with a competitive spirit and an innate rhythm (as well as one of the highest literacy rates per capita) promotes quick-thinking, problem solving, highly-coordinated athletes – also known as climbers.

While in Viñales, we integrated daily with the local climbers at the numerous stalactite-plastered *mogotes,* and nightly at the unadorned rum and salsa music bars. One of my favorite examples of the island-wide culture of reuse occurred daily across from the town square. I curiously approached a group crowded around a man seated at a small wooden

Cuban Ingenuity *Josué Millo bouldering on the wall of his house (left) and "El Expresivo" working out at an improvised weight training facility in Viñales (above).*

table working nimbly with a few worn hand tools and a hissing canister of butane. Amazingly, he was refilling disposable lighters. Each customer would wait less than a minute, exchange a few coins and leave satisfied, truly getting the most out of everything they owned. Another example occurred one evening when our host suggested a spin in his cousin's classic Chevrolet. We all delighted in the shining, hand-brushed paint job and the pieces of aluminum cans used to reinforce the rusted floorboards. It was this improvisational strength of mind that surprised and aligned me with my Cuban climbing compatriots. After all, when you are at the crux of your redpoint burn and you're feeling like you need a patch on your inner-psyche, a refill of your fire, or simply some moxie to get you through to the anchor, know that you are in the land of can-do spirit and what you need is what you got.

Timmy O'Neill - Boulder, Colorado, 2009

PARED DE SILVIA

The Pared de Silvia is diminutive when compared to the massive, cathedral-shaped bay of La Bóveda de las Españolas so, unfortunately, it is often bypassed. But if you take the time to do the five-minute approach and peek behind the trees, you will find a very interesting crag with great lines on solid, shaded rock.

Local Story: Silvia is the name of the farmer that lives across the road from the La Costanera parking lot and she and her two daughters have been extraordinarily generous to the local climbers developing routes on the wall. They have very little, but allow climbers to camp and cook at the house and even deliver hot food to the crag on occasion! The development of La Costanera may not have happened without her help.

APPROACH

If you stand in the parking lot facing the main Costanera wall, Pared de Silvia will be the light coloured wall behind the buildings on your left. The trail starts to the right of the main group of houses, crosses a small dump (hopefully gone soon) and wanders through the trees for another 30 metres before reaching the ledge that forms the base of the crag. The approach takes about five minutes from the parking area.

© YAROBYS GARCÍA

Wasps! *Some of the caves around Viñales provide ideal locations for nest building. Although intimidating, the wasps are generally not very aggressive, except when defending their nests. Some of the routes in this book were built in prime wasp territory (e.g. The Wasp Factory) and the developers went to great lengths to protect themselves and clean the routes so the climbs were free of these stinging inhabitants.*

Da Vinci (7a+) *The rock of the Pared de Slivia is very high quality and always shaded, making it a great venue for hot days. Here, a Ben Iseman tackles the slick initial face of the popular route,* Da Vinci.

THE CLIMBING

The wall is 60-metres tall, but the first 30 metres offer the best climbing. The routes are very interesting and demand a wide range of techniques. Expect tricky cruxes followed by forgiving rests, so push through when in doubt. The rock is of great quality and the features just plead to be climbed. At the time of publication there was still a project waiting to be redpointed.

Pared de Silvía

Routes are listed from right to left.

❶ Caliente 6a+ ★★★ . . . . □

This is the warm-up for the crag, hence the name. The first pitch is bolted.

pitch 1 (6a) Climb the formations to the right of the blank wall, pass the little palm tree and then follow the small caves to the anchor. This pitch can be a little dirty.

pitch 2 (6a+) Climb the face above the belay cave to a big tree with slings that may need replacing. This pitch is rarely climbed due to vegetation and sparsely-placed bolts. Supplement with small Tricams and threads.

2 pitches, mixed *FA: Aníbal Fernández & Abel Pérez, 2002.*

❷ Da Vinci 7a+ ★★★★★ . . . . □

Can you see the knobs? Do you see a line? Follow it and bring your book of tricks because you will find cracks, slabs, tufas and crimps along the full 30 metres of this climb, which ascends the face next to the *Caliente* tufa column.

1 pitch (30 M), 13 bolts *FA: Aníbal Fernández, 2002.*

❸ Coppelia 6c+ ★★★★ . . . . □

Coppelia climbs the next obvious tufa column and has a crux getting to the stalactites. Look around; there is a hidden hold on the right that might help you out!

1 pitch (30 M), bolts *FA: Aníbal Fernández & José Luís Gómez, 2002.*

❹ Filosofia Barata y Zapatos de Goma 7b+ ★★★★ . . . . □

This route starts up the black crack two metres left of *Coppelia*. It has relatively easy climbing with two distinct crux sections.

1 pitch (30 M), 12 bolts *FA: Aníbal Fernández, 2002.*

❺ Entre Mocos 7b+ ★★ . . . . □

This route was an abandoned project located 15 metres left of the routes on the ledge. The crux involves getting over the bouldery sloper below the big tufas. A bolt might be missing.

1 pitch (30 M), 9 bolts *FA: Abel Pérez, 2002.*

Chin Chin Wall

Look for a trail to the right of Pared de Silvía. Routes are listed from left to right.

❻ Chin Chin 7a+ ★★★ . . . . □

This route is right of a cave and was equipped during the climbing festival in 2008.

1 pitch (20 M), 8 bolts *FA: Fransua Bosmerier, Jorge Luís, Raikel Reyes & Yarobys García, 2008.*

❼ Huracán 7c ★★★ . . . . □

Face climbing leads to a crack. Finish at the top of T*ormenta*.

1 pitch (20 M), 8 bolts *FA: Fransua Bosmerier, Jorge Luís, Raikel Reyes & Yarobys García, 2008.*

❽ Tormenta 7b+ ★★★ . . . . □

The last route is on a smaller wall to the right and starts left of a tufa.

1 pitch (22 M), 7 bolts *FA: Fransua Bosmerier, Jorge Luís, Raikel Reyes & Yarobys García, 2008.*

"Chin Chin" wall
PARED DE SILVÍA

CHAPTER 7

OTHER AREAS

Viñales is *the* epicentre of rock climbing in Cuba. Its close proximity to an abundance of high quality stone is found nowhere else in the country. However, Cuba is a geological marvel that is riddled with interesting stone, and potential climbing sites of quality are found from one end of the island to the other. In Pinar del Río province alone, there are at least three valleys with as much potential as Viñales, but the approaches are longer and there are no amenities nearby.

This chapter provides an overview of all the known climbing areas in Cuba. Some cliffs have seen a bit of development and others remain virtually untouched. For climbers willing to stray off the beaten path, Cuba is still a virgin climbing frontier with a ton of development potential. Bring your camping gear and a healthy sense of adventure. The door is wide open...

○ YAROBYS GARCÍA (BOULDERING AT OASIS)

OTHER AREAS

The Cuban climbing areas outlined on the following pages are listed from west to east.

PINAR DEL RÍO

Viñales (1) will always be the focus of climbing in Cuba because the quantity of rock found in the Sierra de los Organos is unrivaled, but these mountains stretch far beyond Viñales. Western Cuba is riddled with limestone walls and caverns; all you need is a car and a keen sense of adventure to find great rock. (Before initiating any development, always check with locals to ensure the area is not restricted.)

The mogotes around the town of **Ancón** (2), 20 kilometres northwest of Viñales, have seen some development by local Cuban climbers and lots of 100-metre-plus walls await the intrepid few. The cliffs are not visible from the road and reaching them involves a 40-minute hike from town, following the river towards El Abra (the pass between Sierra de Galeras and Sierra de Ancón).

Another area worth investigating is the **San Carlos valley** (3), 40 kilometres west of Pinar del Río. This valley is larger than the Viñales area and contains tons of tempting rock. Some routes have been climbed in areas known as Bordallo, Majagua and Calientes, but there is a wealth of untouched, roadside limestone stretching from the small town known as "Cabezas" all the way to the outskirts of Guane.

Finally, west of Viñales in the Municipality of **Minas de Matahambre** (4), routes exist in an area dubbed "La Pimienta". Information can be found on Escaladaencuba.com, but details are vague.

HAVANA

The historic castle of **El Morro** (5), on the opposite side of the Havana harbour, is the weekend climbing hangout for locals. If you want to climb by the sea with a great view of Havana, then check out this unique "crag" for an afternoon after exploring the city. The lead routes have rusty bolts, but there are good toprope anchors (bring long slings).

Forty-five minutes southeast of Havana is an area with some bolted crags and an array of walls and boulders. Follow the highway toward Santa Clara and take the first exit that reads "Tapaste". The majority of developed crags are in a locality known as **"La Jaula"** (6) between the towns of Tapaste and Jaruco and are on the right side of the road.

Also worth exploring are the sea cliffs along the coast east of Havana. Near **Jibacoa beach** (7) and **Santa Cruz del Norte** (8) is some very promising terrain, but so far nothing has been developed.

MATANZAS

There is some bouldering in the **Varadero** (9) area as well as some small sea cliffs, but the rock is very sharp. It's only worth checking out if you are stuck in the most touristy area of Cuba and get bored relaxing on the beach. There is a blog on the Internet posted by a Czech climber that has more information.

Outside the city of **Matanzas** (10) are some small cliffs of reasonable quality. This area has just begun to receive attention from local climbers.

ESCAMBRAY AREA

The mountain range in the centre of the island, known as the **"Sierra del Escambray"** (11), is the second highest in all of Cuba. It is a karst limestone region that hides Cuba's deepest caves and a collection of walls dispersed throughout the mountain's forests. Long approaches in humid conditions are rewarded by some truly spectacular overhangs with waterfalls cascading down the sides. A small selection of routes have been developed, but the area remains problematic in terms of access. On the outskirts of the range, cliffs have been discovered that will likely yield quality climbing as the local community evolves. To climb here, contact the locals through Escaladaencuba.com and check the status of areas like Banao and Fomento.

CAMAGÜEY

This Cuban province was one of the first to see climbing activity in Cuba. The **Sierra de Cubitas** (12) has a plethora of rock and a climber-friendly park management policy. Quality limestone gorges close to one of Cuba's great cities make this area worthy of more attention.

HOLGUIN

With an international airport and an increase in popularity among tourists, **Holguin** (13) could become the next real climbing destination in Cuba. Several cliffs are visible from the road to Guardalavaca beach and the local climbing community, supported by climbers from Havana and Canada, is working on development. Stay tuned.

El Morro

SANTIAGO DE CUBA AND GUANTÁNAMO

If you are a climber visiting Cuba's second largest city, Santiago de Cuba, you should check out the desert-like granite boulder fields of **Oasis** (14), only 20 minutes to the east. To find the blocks, follow the road to Baconao and take the exit to Bucanero Hotel. The boulders are scattered around the small town and in an area called Prado de las Esculturas. There is a lot of potential in this area and it's only been minimally explored by climbers from Havana and Viñales.

Also worthy of serious attention is the entire south coast of Santiago de Cuba and **Guantánamo** (15). This area is littered with limestone and conglomerate cliffs that form terraces stretching down to the sea. The area of primary interest, with the greatest volume of rock, is around Imias and Tortugilla, not far from U.S. naval base, Guantánamo Bay. This is a truly interesting geological area that deserves focused attention. The climbing is close to the ocean (which may yield some deep-water soloing venues) and has a radically different landscape than the lush forests of Viñales.

Last but not least is **Baracoa** (16), the first village settled in Cuba and a true jewel at the east end of the country. The area is incredibly lush and colourful, like nothing else in Cuba, and its large, clear rivers form canyons with steep limestone walls in a very unique setting. Most exploration has been focused around the Yumuri river, east of the city, but many crags abound and it's only a matter of time before climbing finds a niche in this outdoor paradise.

El Morro

BILINGUAL GLOSSARY

The following bilingual glossary provides a brief summary of the most common English language climbing terms and their approximate Cuban-Spanish equivalents.

anchor	reunión, fisuero enpotradore
artificial	artificial
bees	avejas
Belay off!	Libre! Me puedes soltar!
belay (place)	reunión
belay device	placa
belay (v)	dar seguridad
bolt	parabolt, spit
boulder	bloque
bouldering	búlder
carabiner	mosquetón
carabiner, locking	mosquetón con seguridad
cave	cueva, caverna
chalk	magnesio
clean	limpio
climb (v)	escalar
climb (signal)	cuando quiera
climbing	escalando
clip (v)	mosquetonear
column	colada (large), paleta (medium), costilla (small)
corner	diedro
crack	fisura, grieta (large)
drill bit	barrena

drill	taladro (n), taladrar (v)
exposed	expuesta
face	placa
farmer	guajiro
first ascentionists	aperturistas, primeros ascensionistas
first aid kit	biotiquin, primeros auxilios
fixed anchors	estación fija
foothold	presa de pie
forest	bosque, monte
free	libre
friends/cams	frends
grade/rating	grado
guide (person)	guía
guidebook	guía
guided trek	excursión con guia
hammer	martillos, maza
handhold	presa
hanger	placa, chapa
hanging	colgante
harness	arnés
helmet	casco
hex	hexentrix
holds	agarres
insecticide (for wasps)	polvo duble o polvo piojillo

jugs/juggy	canto, mucho canto	**rope**	cuerda, soga
lead	puntear (v), el punteo (the lead)	**route**	vía, ruta
ledge	repisa	**route, sport**	vía equipado, rutas deportivas
limestone	caliza	**route, gear**	vía tradicional
Lower me!	Bajame!	**route, single pitch (lower off)**	con descuelge
map	mapa	**Slack!**	Cuerda!
mountain range	mogotes, sierra	**slings**	expres, cinta
mono pocket	monodedo	**sloper**	romo
nuts (all types)	fisureros, tuercas	**smooth**	liso
overhang	desplome o extraplomo	**snake**	maja
overhanging	desplomado	**stalactites**	estalactitas
overhangs	desploma, estraploma	**steep**	escarpado, empinado
pack	mochila	**stoppers**	estoper
pinch (n)	pinza	**Take!**	Tensión!
pitch	largo	**Tension!**	Tensión!
pond	presa, laguna	**traditional**	clasica, tradicional
protection	protección, seguridades intermedias	**trail**	trillo, pista, sendero, camino
pumpy	mucho pumpito	**tree**	arbol, mata, palo
put up	abrir (open)	**Tricam**	Tricam
rappel	rápel	**tufas**	chorreras
rest (stance)	reposo, descanso	**vertical**	vertical
road, dirt	guardarralla	**wall**	pared, paredes
rock	roca	**wasp**	avispa
roof	techo	**water**	agua

Aníbal Fernández was born in 1980 in Havana, Cuba, and has been fascinated with the outdoors for the better part of his life. In his early teens, Aníbal got involved with Cuba's Caving Society and took many adventurous trips around the country, including exhilarating river descents and deep cave explorations. It was with the members of this club that he learned about ropes, carabiners, risk management and living outside – the skills necessary to tackle the initial development of rock climbing in Cuba. Since those first exploratory years, Aníbal has been involved in every stage of Cuban climbing development: exploring new areas for potential, pioneering many first ascents, introducing safe climbing techniques, organizing gear donations from foreigners and, most importantly, motivating an entire generation of locals to adopt a new lifestyle! Since leaving Cuba, Aníbal has climbed extensively in North America and Europe and has hundreds of first ascents under his belt, as well as a Rock Guide certification from Exum Mountain Guides. He currently resides in Toronto, Canada, with his wife, Kerry, and dog, Oso, far from the subtropical jungles of his youth. Living "up north" has taught him how to climb with fingers numbed by cold stone, sling up a bear bag while camping, and wait patiently for his next climbing trip. He feels strongly connected to the climbing in Cuba and returns annually for the magnificent stone.

Armando Menocal was born in the U.S., but his roots and heart are in Cuba. His great-grandmother was a cousin of Mario García-Menocal, a rebel who fought to liberate Cuba from Spanish rule and governed the country from 1912–1921. Armando now works as an independent advocate after years of running a public interest law firm in San Francisco (and moonlighting as a guide). Along the way, he founded The Access Fund, the largest organization of climbers in America. In 2009, he started Access Pan America, a grassroots effort of climbers, organizations, and corporate supporters tasked with keeping climbing areas open and protecting the environment in all the Western Hemisphere. *Outside* magazine called Armando, "a world-class Wyoming climber who's been helping the Cuban rock-climbing community get off the ground". In 1998, Armando travelled to Cuba in search of his family roots, and chanced on Viñales instead. Amazed at the potential, he made dozens of return trips to develop routes and eventually created Cubaclimbing.com to publicize Cuba to the world. A decade of activism has left an independent Cuban climbing community, free of control or dependence, and the primary developers of climbing in Cuba. It also resulted in Armando being banned from Cuba. Today, he is attached to Cuba by more than just the rope, and hopes that one day he will be able to return to Viñales.